VOICES FROM SLAVERY

The Life and Beliefs of African Slaves in Britain

Chigor Chike

Bloomington, IN  Milton Keynes, UK

authorHOUSE®

AuthorHouse™
1663 Liberty Drive, Suite 200
Bloomington, IN 47403
www.authorhouse.com
Phone: 1-800-839-8640

AuthorHouse™ UK Ltd.
500 Avebury Boulevard
Central Milton Keynes, MK9 2BE
www.authorhouse.co.uk
Phone: 08001974150

This book is a work of non-fiction. Unless otherwise noted, the author
and the publisher make no explicit guarantees as to the accuracy of
the information contained in this book and in some cases, names
of people and places have been altered to protect their privacy.

First published by AuthorHouse 1/29/2007

ISBN: 978-1-4259-8739-8 (sc)

Printed in the United States of America
Bloomington, Indiana

This book is printed on acid-free paper.

To my parents

Onwo and Akanene

CONTENTS

FOREWORD

H ow readily we use shorthand expressions like the word 'slaves'. This has the effect of depersonalising the individuals involved. We are therefore indebted to Chigor Chike for taking the time to produce this book, to remind us that each of the estimated 30 million Africans who were taken into slavery, during what I prefer to call the European Slave Trade, was an individual with personality, hopes, fears, opinions, beliefs and a God-given potential. Each was a human being made in the image of God, never merely a slave.

Chike uses four well-known names from the period to demonstrate the humanity of all enslaved Africans. In their different ways, Ignatius Sancho, Ukawsaw Gronniosaw, Olaudah Equiano and Ottobah Cugoano help us to understand that oppression can never completely squash the human spirit, it merely suppresses it. And that even in the most inhumane circumstances, light overcomes darkness, hope outlasts despair and good triumphs over evil.

The thoughts and expressions of these four witnesses, described by Chikerespectively as poet, noble, activist and visionary, come alive on these pages as we are taken on a journey through their insights on Christianity, God, humanity and slavery. They show us the manner in which people can retain their God-given abilities to think and act in the face of adversity. They also demonstrate a diversity of thoughts and attitudes. Based on the wealth of what we have here, we can but ponder the enormous loss to the sum of human knowledge and enrichment of those whose lives were cut short or suppressed so that their 'voices' might go unheard.

We have much to learn from these four heroes and the ways they came to terms with the context in which they fatefully found themselves. Take for example the eloquence Sancho expresses in his writings; eloquence gained in the face of opposition that attempted to keep him from learning to read. His self motivation conquered that hindrance. Similarly, Gronniosaw did not allow his poverty to hinder his tendencies towards nobility. Then, at a time when slaves were expected to be seen but not heard, Equiano excelled as a political activist, playing a significant part in the abolitionist movement. Finally, there is Cugoano, unafraid to utilise theological language in the service of liberation for a better future for the enslaved and their enslavers. Oh that today, we could discover such boldness of spirit to be prophetic in the face of injustice and inhumanity.

Throughout this book, Christian principles are highlighted, such as faith, prayer, liberation, compassion, charity, equality, diversity and love. So too is that forthrightness for calling a spade a spade. So, in an expression of tough love and truth-speaking; slave traders are called 'robbers and heinous transgressors' against their fellow humanity. May be the most compelling lesson of this book is the understanding gained from these four, symbolic as they are of millions more, that no amount of perpetrated wickedness can remove from the human spirit that sense of being made in the divine image. Hope springs eternal in the human soul, for liberation and for justice. 'Slave' is an inappropriate term to apply to these men; they were first and foremost men created in God's image.

Bishop Dr Joe Aldred
Secretary, Minority Ethnic Christian Affairs
Churches Together in England

PREFACE

It was about 1994 when I first heard about Africans who had lived in Britain as slaves. That was just a few years after I came to Britain from my native Nigeria. The more I read about them, the more fascinated I became with their stories. But I was struck by how little people knew about this group. To my surprise, I found a lack of knowledge about these Africans of the slavery era among people in Britain, both black and white. Since I learnt about this group, I have used every opportunity to write about them, so that many other people would know and understand about their lives. Over time, I have become convinced that what was needed was a book dedicated to them.

This is therefore a book on African slaves and not a book on the subject of slavery. The intention is to focus on the Africans as individuals. It will not, however, be a chronological description of their lives. Rather, we will be looking at their views on different issues, and where appropriate, illustrate the role that their life experiences played in shaping those views. We will look, for example, at their views on Christianity, humanity and God. We will also look at their attitudes toward their enslavement, since this was a dominant issue in their lives. The book begins with a brief description of slavery and the slave trade in order to give a wider context to the individual stories. The book is not, however, intended to give a comprehensive description of slavery and the slave trade.

My hope is that readers will find this book useful at different levels. They will learn about four human beings who had quite difficult lives and who, in order to survive, developed their own ways of coping. The book will be useful for the insight it gives into the lives of individuals experiencing slavery. Quite often in contemporary writing, slavery and the slave trade are discussed in broad terms, highlighting the huge numbers of Africans sold and used and the huge wealth this brought to the traders. Rarely discussed are the points of view of the individuals sold and used as slaves. This book intends to contribute to this neglected area. It will shed light, from the perspective of the individual slave, on prevailing social and philosophical concepts, such as identity, racism and the place of religion in individual and national life. These are important issues today, as countries around the world become more and more ethnically diverse.

The book might also make another important correction. Much of the discussion in Europe of the abolition of the slave trade omits the contribution of Africans, focusing more on the work of European abolitionists. But in so framing the story, we do a disservice not only to history but to the European abolitionists, who saw their African comrades as equal contributors. Those European abolitionists would see the omission of their African partners in the record of the fight against the slave trade as the resurfacing of the very oppression of black people that they devoted so much energy to fight against. Such omissions also create a view of history that does not allow important lessons to be learnt. The book will show how over time, some Africans who got back their freedom used it to fight for the freedom of other slaves. Through their letters, newspaper articles, Christian ideas or memoirs, the writings of these individuals made an important contribution to the fight for the abolition of slavery and the slave trade.

In writing this book, I have been greatly inspired by these Africans slaves and ex-slaves. Being African myself, I found they meant more to me than mere subjects for detached academic study. The fact that I live in London, where all the four people we will be looking at lived at some point, increases my connection with them. My residence in London also gave me the opportunity to use the British Library, which has the original works of Sancho, Gronniosaw, Equiano and Cugoano. The feeling I had when I handled these originals for the first time is something I will remember for some time. I am also grateful to the people who have researched these stories and through whose work I and many others have come to know about these Africans. In this regard, I particularly want to pay tribute to Paul Edwards for his contribution towards putting these stories into wide circulation in the modern era. I have made use of the work of Edwards and Polly Rewt on Sancho's letters to assign names to the characters referred to in the letters. These names are often represented as mere initials in Sancho's original manuscript.

I would like to thank David Whitehead, for patiently reading through the manuscript and making both grammatical and structural suggestions; Kofi Bonney and Kevin Allison, for reading through the final draft; Marvis Cudjoe and Tina Dugard, for their help with the illustrations; and others who helped me in other ways. I would also like to thank the staff of Author House for the help and guidance they gave me through the publishing process. Finally, I would like to thank Obi and the children for their patience and support.

COVER/ILLUSTRATIONS

Top Left

Portrait of Ignatius Sancho. Reproduced with the permission of the National Gallery of Canada.

Top Right

A drawing of Ukawsaw Gronniosaw, which is on the cover of the 1811 edition of his book. Reproduced with the permission of the British Library.

Bottom Left

"Ottobah Cugoano" by Tina Dugard © Chigor Chike. Artist impression commissioned by Chigor Chike based on existing information and image of Ottobah Cugoano. Richard Cosway's drawing of an African servant believed to be Cugoano is reproduced inside this book, with the permission of the Whitworth Gallery, University of Manchester.

Bottom Right (in red coat)

Portrait, traditionally believed to be that of Olaudah Equiano; reproduced with the permission of the Royal

Albert Memorial Gallery, Exeter. Recent scholarship has cast some doubt on the identity of this sitter. Another portrait of Equiano is reproduced inside this book. The second portrait comes from Equiano's book, the *Interesting Narrative*, so it is incontrovertibly him. It has been reproduced here with the permission of the British Library.

CHAPTER 1:

INTRODUCTION

The slavery of Africans in their millions for hundreds of years is, by any measure, one of worst atrocities that human beings have carried out till this day. From about the mid-fifteenth century, Europeans were buying and selling Africans as slaves. It began when the Portuguese and the Spanish who established trade links with Africa decided that it was more profitable to capture Africans and take them back with them to Europe to sell, rather than returning with empty ships. With the discovery of the American continent by Europeans, these same countries now diverted their sale of Africans to that continent to supply the many plantations requiring manual labourers. Some British ships were involved in selling slaves to the Spanish colonies, but the British joined the trade proper after they established their own colonies and wanted slaves to work at their plantations. By all accounts, the British, when they joined, not only dominated the trade but expanded it. In the peak of the slave trade era, the British carried more slaves from Africa to America than all the other countries put together. Hundreds of ships were leaving from Bristol, Liverpool and London to buy and sell Africans.

They developed what was called the Triangular Trade, whereby the ships left British ports with British-made goods like textiles, muskets, gunpowder and spirits; the traders would sell these goods in Africa, then buy Africans, who they would sell as slaves in America, where they then buy such goods as sugar, rum and tobacco which they would bring back to Britain to sell. In Britain, they would use some of the profit to buy more manufactured goods and the cycle would begin all over again. Not only the cities of Bristol and Liverpool, but the whole country benefited from this. The writer Peter Fryer writes:

> It was an ingenious system, for ships never needed to travel empty. And it was an enormously profitable system for the planters whose slaves produced the sugar, the merchant capitalists who sold them the slaves, the industrial capitalists who supplied the manufactured goods with which the slaves were bought, and the bankers and commission agents who lent money to all of them.[1]

Many historians believe that the profits of the slave trade were of major importance in the formation of the capital required to launch the British Industrial Revolution.[2]

For most Africans who ended up as slaves, their life in slavery began when they were kidnapped from their village. The raids to kidnap Africans were, at the early period of the trade era, carried out by the Europeans themselves.

But over time, there emerged African middlemen who paid other Africans to raid villages. The captured person's journey to the coast depended on how far inland they were captured. When they reached the coast, usually in poor health, they were sold and stored in one of many forts (or castles) built by European merchants over the period, and then into ships. One such castle, which is now a World Heritage site, was called Elmina. A recent visitor to Elmina, which was one of twenty castles used for slave trading on the coast of what is now Ghana, writes:

> Not knowing what awaited them on the slave ships, those who made it to the coast were held captives in the castle's dungeons. They were subjected to all sorts of indignities, intimidation and torture. They were shackled in the damp and dark dungeons. It is said that up to three hundred captives were packed into each dungeon, without room to even lift an arm or move around. Food was scarce and disease was rampant.
>
> The unsanitary conditions under which the captives lived were unbelievable. Without room to breathe properly in those dungeons, the captives had to defecate there. The sick were often not attended to, and many of them died while held captives there. Air quality wasn't a priority. The stench in those dungeons must have been nauseating. Even today, the dungeons still reek.[3]

Life aboard the ships was equally bad, as most captains tried to pack in as many slaves as possible. Many people on board, slaves and crew, did not make it through the journey to America – a journey commonly known as the Middle Passage. A common killer was dysentery. When they arrived in America, some Africans ended up in the Caribbean, many got sold on further north to present day US. The vast majority of the slaves worked in plantations of sugar and tobacco. Life expectancy was very low, especially for the field slaves, because their owners were mainly interested in extracting as much labour from them as possible before they died. They were simply worked to death by their owners, who would easily restock with new slaves from Africa. In the sugar plantations in the West Indies, the slaves were divided into three gangs depending on their strength. The first gang were the plantations' "shock troops", who did the heavy work; the second gang, made of people like mothers of suckling children, did gentler work; and the third gang, made of the very young and the old, serviced the workers.[4] The historian, James Walvin, described this as: "A highly efficient labour system designed to squeeze from them the maximum of effort. It was also a key method for the control and discipline of crowds of slaves".[5]

Some slaves worked as domestic servants and, generally, lived under less harsh conditions. Some were taken by their masters to Britain or other European countries to work as domestic servants, so they escaped not only the hard labour of field work, but also the harsh conditions of West Indian slavery.

Even though the plantations were in the far away Caribbean, many plantations were owned by British people. Many ordinary British people also had investments in the shipping companies trading in slaves. In the late 1700s, the conscience of many British people was stirred regarding what was been done to their fellow human beings. The campaign for abolition of the slave trade began. A key event was a meeting held by a group that was mainly made up of Quakers in 1787 which launched the campaign against abolition. Before then, Granville Sharp had been fighting in the law courts for the freedom of black people in Britain. At the centre of the 1787 meeting was Thomas Clarkson, who would go on to work tirelessly for abolition. That group, which was called the Committee for Abolition of the African Slave Trade, helped to persuade William Wilberforce to join the cause, and he became the leader of the fight in the British Parliament.

But the abolition movement was more than a parliamentary affair; it was a mass movement. In the black community, there was a group of black abolitionists called the Sons of Africa, who lobbied MPs, and collaborated with Sharp, Clarkson and other white abolitionists. The leader of that group was Olaudah Equiano, who was born in present day Nigeria, but who, after years of slavery, had bought his freedom. Equiano's book, *The Interesting Narrative of Olaudah Equiano*, which ran into many editions during his lifetime, was one of the biggest literary blows to the slave trade. The book, Equiano's campaigning tours of Britain and Ireland, and his newspaper articles challenging supporters of the trade made him one of the biggest contributors to the cause of abolition. Another key member of that group was Ottobah Cugoano, who, in 1787 (the same year the Quakers launched their campaign in London) published a book entitled *Thoughts and*

Sentiments on the Evil of Slavery. It was a comprehensive criticism of slavery from a Christian point of view. In 1807, the abolitionists, white and black, won the fight as a bill was passed in Parliament to abolish the trade. Slavery continued in the British colonies, however, until 1838.

As one would imagine, accurate records of the number of Africans transported to a life of slavery in America are difficult to arrive at. The number of those who made it to America alive over the 300 years of the trade has been estimated to be about 15 million. No wonder it has been described as "one of the greatest involuntary migrations of all time."[6] It is also widely believed that as many Africans died in the trading process as actually got to America. Many died during the long, arduous journey from interior African villages to the coast; more died while being held in the dungeons at the coastal forts; and many more died aboard the ships on the journey to America. So the slave trade might have depleted the population of Africa by close to 30 million. Another approach taken by historians has been to look at the total effect of slavery on the population of Africa. In 1850, at the end of the slave trade, the population of Africa was about 25 million. Many historians believe that without the slave trade, it could have been up to 53 million. [7]

This Book

The sheer number of Africans killed, sold and used as slaves can hide the fact that these were individual people, each of whom have their own story. That fact, coupled with the tendency among Western historians to focus on white personalities when writing about the slavery era means that the stories of individual black people are often neglected. The intention of this book is to address that neglect by shining the spotlight on four African slaves. We will hear from the four what life in slavery was like. We have chosen the four best-known black people who lived in Britain during the era of slavery – Ignatius Sancho, Ukawsaw Gronniosaw, Olaudah Equiano and Ottobah Cugoano. We will explore through their own words what their attitude was to slavery, humanity, Christianity and God. Each chapter will end with an imaginary presentation by the four on the particular subject of the chapter. We will conclude the book with a short discussion of the relevance of their views for some of the social and political issues facing people in Britain today. For example, what insights does their experience bring into debates about identity and culture of the different communities that live in Britain today? How does their experience of the Christian religion enlighten debates about what place religion should have in national life? What similarities are there between slavery and racism? These are some of the questions that will be encountered in the following pages.

The style of the book is one which allows the reader to hear from the slaves as directly as possible, in order that the reader can get the direct impact of the individual slave's own style of writing. Expect to be entertained by the poetry Sancho displays in his letters. For example, after receiving a letter from a young lady, Sancho wrote back, "I protest, my dear Madam, there is nothing so dangerous to the calm philosophical temper of fifty – as a friendly epistle from a pretty young woman".[8] After more pleasant remarks, he added his gratitude, "But I did not mean to write a starch complimentary letter – and I believe you will think I have flourished rather too much. Here then – I recover my wits – and the first use I make of them is to thank you".[9]

The reader might also notice the childlike faith of Gronniosaw; a faith that appears to grow stronger at the face of adversity. Once, after reflecting on a difficult summer, he remarked, "The boundless goodness of God to me… I have been wonderfully supported in every affliction. My God never left me, I perceived light still thro' the thickest darkness".[10]

Some of the words might make for uncomfortable reading. For example, we might be saddened or challenged by some of Equiano's words, as he narrates his life story and reflects on it. Take for example, this description of what went on aboard a slave ship he worked on while still a slave, himself:

> When we have had some of these slaves on board my master's vessel to carry them to other islands, or to America, I have known our mates to commit these acts most shamefully, to the disgrace, not of Christians only, but of men. I have even known them gratify their brutal passion with females not ten years old; and these abominations some of them practiced to such scandalous excess, that one of our captains discharged the mate and others on that account. And yet in Montserrat I have seen a negro man staked to the ground, and cut most shockingly, and then his ears cut off bit by bit, because he had

been connected with a white woman who was a common prostitute.[11]

Equiano thus observed the contradiction whereby it was a crime for a black man to sleep with a white woman, even if that woman was a prostitute, but there was nothing wrong in white men violating African children under ten.

Finally, we might notice the complexity of Cugoano's thoughts and his wide knowledge of the Bible. For example, he pointed out that those people who refer to occurances of slavery in the Bible to justify slavery in the world were using the Bible wrongly. In his view, to use the Bible in the right way is not simply a question of *method* but a question of *outcome.* To use the Bible to justify evil is wrong, no matter how clever the method employed in the process:

> The pretences that some men make use of for holding of slaves, must be evidently the grossest perversion of reason, and a wrong use or disbelief of the sacred writings, when any thing found there is so perverted by them, and set up as a precedent and rule for men to commit wickedness. They had better have no reason, and no belief in the scriptures, and make no use of them at all, than only to believe, and make use of that which leads them into the most abominable evil and wickedness of dealing unjustly with their fellow men.[12]

Chapter 2:
Meet the
Characters

In this chapter, we will describe the four people whose voices we will hear in this book, namely, Ignatius Sancho, Ukawsaw Gronniosaw, Olaudah Equiano and Ottobah Cugoano. As happens to slaves, these men were known by other names, usually European names, during their slavery. Gronniosaw was known by the English name James Albert, Equiano was known as Gustavus Vassa and Cugoano was known by the European name John Stuart. But we will use their African names throughout this book. Of the four men, we can easily put them into two pairs. The first two, Sancho and Gronniosaw, lived before the peak period of the fight for abolition of the slave trade and so that subject featured little in their writing. Equiano and Cugoano, on the other hand, were at the very centre of that fight. For each man, we will give some biographical details, describe some of their activities and also say something about their books.

Ignatius Sancho

Ignatius Sancho

Ignatius Sancho was born on a slave ship in the mid-Atlantic in 1729. His mother died shortly after they reached land and his father killed himself rather than live as a slave.[13] Sancho was brought to England by his owner when he was about two and was given to three sisters who lived in Greenwich. In fact, it was the sisters that gave him what became his surname, Sancho, because they thought he looked like the squire (i.e., a man-at-arms in the service of another) in the Spanish novel, *Don Quixote*.[14] The three sisters wanted to keep him uneducated but Sancho taught himself to read and write.[15] He was helped in this respect by a family friend to the sisters, the Duke of Montagu, who gave him presents of books.[16] He would later go to serve the Montagu family, and when he retired from their service due to ill health and old age, he set up a grocery shop in Charles Street, Westminster, with his own savings and with money from the Montagu family. He worked in this shop for the rest of his life, helped by his wife, Ann, a black woman from the Caribbean, with whom he had six children.

What sets Sancho apart from our other three characters is the elegance of his writing. Indeed, we can nickname him "Sancho the Poet". This is because even though all four were writers in their own way, for Sancho, writing was an art to be enjoyed and he wrote with remarkable elegance. He was the first African prose writer whose work was published in England.[17] His book, entitled *Letters of the Late Ignatius Sancho*, a collection of letters he had written mostly to friends, was published in 1782, two years after his death. The book proved to be an immediate bestseller and would be republished several times in years to come. In fact, the reason for the publication of his book was not particularly for its content but for the beautiful way that Sancho expressed himself – to show the British public that an African could possess such skills. Here are some examples. The first is from a letter he wrote to a friend upon the death of the son of the Duke of Montagu:

> Time will, I hope, bring them comforts. Their loss is great indeed; and not to them only. The public have a loss – Goodness – Wisdom – Knowledge – and Greatness – were united in him. Heaven has gained an Angel; but earth has lost a treasure.[18]

The second example comes from a letter he wrote to the son of a friend who was overseas:. After beginning with, "Your good father insists on my scribbling a sheet of absurdities, and gives me a notable reason for it, that is, 'Jack will be pleased with it'",[19] he writes this postscript:

> It is with sincere pleasure I hear you have a lucrative establishment – which will enable you to appear and act with decency - Your good sense will naturally lead you to proper economy – as distant from frigid parsimony, as from heedless extravagancy – But as you may possibly have some time to spare upon your hands for necessary recreation, give me leave to obtrude my poor advice – I have heard it more than once observed of fortunate adventurers – they have come home enriched in purse, but wretchedly barren in intellects.[20]

But writing was not the only thing Sancho engaged in. He also wrote poems and plays and composed music. Some of his music was broadcast by the BBC as recently as 1958. In his later life, Sancho was very much an accepted member of the literary circle in London. Records show that writers and painters sought his opinion on their work.[21]

Letters of the Late Ignatius Sancho An African sold out quickly after publication. It is important to bear in mind that this is a collection of letters which Sancho wrote to friends. That means that it may not represent the full range of subjects that were giving him concern – only the ones that he had the occasion to write to his friends about. The selection of his letters for publication was made after his death by a family friend, who may have had her own reasons for including or leaving out some letters from the collection. Apart from these considerations, the collection gives an important insight into Sancho's thoughts. Or put another way, it remains a valuable means for people today to hear the voice of this African slave.

Ukawsaw Gronniosaw

Ukawsaw Gronniosaw

The second slave voice comes from a man called Ukawsaw Gronniosaw. If Sancho was distinguished from the others by his writing, Gronniosaw was distinguished by his poverty. Even for a slave, he lived a life of remarkable destitution. Ironically, of the four Africans, Gronniosaw started out in the best position. He was born in Bornu, West of Lake Chad in the northeast part of present-day Nigeria.[22] His mother was eldest daughter of the king of Zaara and he was the youngest of six children.[23] So he was born into the nobility of Africa. Gronniosaw's story suggests that when he left his homeland, he did not do so as a slave.

It all began one rainy day when a mysterious event left Gronniosaw, aged 15, depressed. Nothing his family did helped his situation. Then a merchant offered to help. Gronniosaw gave this account:

> About that time there came a merchant from the Gold Coast (the third city in Guinea). He traded with the inhabitants of our country in ivory and he took great notice of my unhappy situation and inquired into the cause. He expressed vast concern for me and said, if my parents would part with me for a little while, and let him take me home with him, it would be of more service to me than anything they could do for me. He told me that if I would go with him, I should see houses with wings to them walk upon water [possible reference to ships]; and should also see the white folks; and that he had many sons nearly of my age, which should be my companions; and he added to all this, that he

would bring me safe back again soon. I was highly pleased with the account of this strange place, and was very desirous of going.[24]

It all went wrong when he got to the man's house in the Gold Coast (at least 1,000 kilometres away from Gronniosaw's home). The ruling chief of the area, when he discovered Gronniosaw was the grandson of the king of Bornu, accused him of spying and wanted to kill him. To save him from this, his host sold him to the captain of a Dutch ship.[25] As he was sold from master to master, he found himself in the Caribbean, North America and England. It was in England that he took the name for which he is sometimes known, James Albert.[26] At different times, he lived in London, Colchester, Norwich and Kidderminster. He served in the British Army in 1762.

Gronniosaw showed nobility of a different kind by the way he treated the family of one of his masters. The man in question was a religious minister in New York, Mr. Freelandhouse, who not only taught Gronniosaw how to read and write but upon his death left some money in his will for Gronniosaw and his freedom. Gronniosaw stayed with his mistress, Mrs. Freelandhouse, and with the sons of she and her husband after she also died, even though he was free by that time. But he paid for this because when the man's children died, Gronniosaw was left destitute. He left New York for England but his fortunes did not improve much after he came to England. At times, both he and his wife, Betty, were unemployed and the family had nothing to eat. Once, when they had no food whatsoever, he got four carrots from a gardener and the family had to eat one a day so that the carrots did not run out before they could find other food. He was helped at different points in his life by a number of people. Once, he was helped by a lawyer from Colchester who gave him a guinea and employed him for a year[27] and, at another time, he was helped by a Quaker who paid his rent and thus saved his family from eviction.

Gronniosaw's book, which we will discuss in more detail, is called *The Narrative of the Most Remarkable Life of James Albert Ukawsaw Gronniosaw An African Prince* and was published in 1770. Unlike Sancho, Gronniosaw did not write his book in the strict sense. Rather, he dictated it to somebody described as "a young lady of the town of Leominster".[28] This may be important because it might have influenced, if only in a little way, what Gronniosaw said or did not say. It is also possible that, having experienced so much hardship, and finding himself in a position where his story and views were of interest to the predominantly white public, Gronniosaw might have avoided jeopardizing that opportunity by expressing views that could be seen as radical. We will see, for example, that his views on slavery are in many ways different from those of the likes of Equiano and Cugoano, our remaining two voices.

Olaudah Equiano

Olaudah Equiano

Olaudah Equiano has been the best known of our four characters, both during his day and ever since. He has been described as the first political leader of Britain's black community.[29] Equiano was an Igbo, born in the eastern part of present day Nigeria. He was one of seven children and was said to be his mother's favourite. At 11, he and his sister were sold into slavery. Here is Equiano's account of how this happened:

> One day, when all our people were gone out to their works as usual, and only I and my dear sister were left to mind the house, two men and a woman got over our walls, and in a moment seized us both, and, without giving us time to cry out or make resistance, they stopped our mouths and ran off with us into the nearest wood. Here they tied our hands, and continued to carry us as far as they could, till night came on, when we reached a small house, where the robbers halted for refreshment and spent the night.[30]

It took about six months of travelling for Equiano to get to the coast to be transported to the Americas. In that time he would be separated from his sister, reunited briefly once, and once more separated, never to see her again. After a fortnight in Barbados, he was sold to a man who lived in what is now US. From there he was bought by a British Naval officer called Pascal, who he served for many years.[31] Two sisters called Guerin, who were relatives of Pascal, and with whom Equiano stayed

in London, taught him to read. But Pascal later betrayed
Equiano by selling him to another owner, when Equiano
thought that all his earning on the side, which he gave to
Pascal, had bought him his freedom. After more years as
a slave, Equiano's hard work paid off as he saved enough
money to buy his freedom. He later settled in London and
spent the rest of his life fighting tirelessly for the abolition
of the slave trade.

Equiano's anti-slavery activities can be traced back
to 1767 when he tried to stop the transportation from
Britain to St Kitts of a freed slave called John Annis,
whose former master had arranged to have him kidnapped from Britain.[32] When a scheme was set up
by the government to send freed slaves back to Sierra
Leone, Equiano discovered the organizers were doing
it badly and with little regard to the wellbeing of the
black people and he reported them to the authorities.[33]
In the years that followed, in the words of Peter Fryer,
Equiano, "emerged as a capable and energetic publicist:
a fluent writer and speaker, a campaigner prepared to
travel wherever he was invited to present the abolitionist case".[34] Between 1789 and 1793, he went on speaking tours to Birmingham, Manchester, Nottingham,
Sheffield, Cambridge, Durham, Stockton, Hull, Bath
and Devizes. He toured Ireland for eight months and
also toured Scotland, where he got many subscribers for
his book. He wrote many articles for London newspapers, often countering the argument of those who were
campaigning for the slave trade to continue.[35] In 1783, he
called Granville Sharpe's attention to the mass murder of
132 black slaves who were thrown alive into the sea by the

Liverpool slave ship, Zong.[36] When the anti-slavery bill was going through Parliament, The MPs behind it frequently consulted him, and he would go with other leaders of the black community in Britain to Westminster to listen to the debates. Regarding that matter, he met with both the Speaker of the House of Commons and the Prime Minister.[37]

Equiano's book, which will be our main source for his story and remarks is entitled *Interesting Narrative of the Life of Olaudah Equiano, or Gustavus Vassa, the African.* This is essentially an autobiography, and a very powerful one. Fryer gave this description of the book and its effect in Britain:

> The most important single literary contribution to the campaign for abolition. For the first time the case for abolition, presented by a black writer in a popular form, reached a wide reading public. It was, for instance, the last secular book read by Wesley before his death.[38]

The Interesting Narrative was very effective in rousing public interest and went through eight editions in Equiano's own lifetime. On one of his speaking tours, somebody told him that he was having more effect on the cause for abolition "than half the people in the country".[39]

This was probably said in jest and may have been an exaggeration. What is not in doubt is that Equiano was one of the most influential people in the fight for abolition. In his own lifetime, he was recognized as a spokesperson for the black community. It is an indication of the racism in the recording of the history of Britain that Equiano is little known to British people today. In this respect, one salutes the courage and fairness of people like Paul Edwards, James Walvin and Peter Fryer, who have worked against the tide to bring these stories to the people of today. In so doing, these white men reflect the way in which Equiano worked with both black and white people in the abolition fight. It is probably fair to say he was to the anti-slavery movement what Martin Luther King Jr was to the American Civil Rights movement. In his early fifties, Equiano was struck down by illness. And in a wicked irony of life, the man whose first name, "Olaudah," means "a resounding voice," lost his voice due to illness. He died at 52 on 31st March 1797, ten years before abolition became law. Equiano was in that sense like the Biblical Moses, who led the Israelites out of Egypt but died before they got to the Promised Land. Equiano, having worked hard for black people to get to the "promised land" of abolition, died before it became a reality.

Ottobah Cugoano

The last of our four characters is Quobna Ottobah Cugoano. Cugoano was not only a contemporary of Equiano but a good friend of his. He was involved with Equiano in the fight for abolition, but was, in his own right, one of the leaders of Britain's black community. Cugoano was born about the year 1757 in the Fante area of what is now Ghana. His first name, Quobna (spelt "Kwobena" in Fante language) means "born on Tuesday"; but it was by his middle name, Ottobah, that he was more commonly known. At the age of 13, Cugoano was kidnapped one day when he was playing with other children in the woods. Cugoano gave this account of that event:

> We had not been above two hours before our troubles began, when several great ruffians came upon us suddenly, and said we had committed a fault against their lord, and we must go and answer ourselves before him. Some of us attempted in vain to run away, but pistols and cutlasses were soon introduced, threatening, that if we offered to stir we should all lie dead on the spot.

The kidnappers were, of course, lying and they used this lie time and again as they travelled day after day towards the ship that would take them out of Africa. Cugoano passed through America and after about two years, in the year 1772, ended up in England. His owner who brought him to England freed him. Cugoano changed his name to John Stewart (or Stuart) to avoid being sold back into slavery.[40] He lived most of his life in London

"'The Artist and his Wife in a Garden, with a black Servant" [P.20239], Cosway, Servant is believed to be Ottobah Cugoano and was married to an English woman. Somebody who knew him when he was about 40 described him as pious, gentle, of modest character, honest in manner and very talented.[41]

Cugoano was actively involved in the affairs of many Africans living in London in his day. He was a staunch campaigner for abolition, working closely with white abolitionist Granville Sharp.[42] In 1786 Cugoano played a part in the rescue of Henry Demane, a black man who had been kidnapped and was being shipped to the West Indies. Cugoano reported the matter to Granville Sharpe, who made a legal intervention.[43] Apart from his campaign, he was something of a visionary. He made suggestions on the slave issue which were well before his time. Fryer has pointed out that Cugoano was the first writer in English to declare that the slaves had not only the moral right but the moral duty to resist slavery. His statement will considered more fully in a later chapter. He also proposed, twenty years before it was actually done, that a fleet of ships be deployed to the Atlantic to stop ships carrying Africans away into slavery.[44] He also predicted that the evil trade in human beings would be ended by a revolution, because that is what tends to happen in history. "History affords us many examples of severe retaliations, revolutions and dreadful overthrows...what revolution the end of that predominant evil of slavery and oppression may produce".[45]

This prophesy was remarkable for the fact that he made it four years before there was a slave revolt in Haiti and two years before a revolution took place in France.[46] He was, probably, the first person, white or black, to demand

publicly the total abolition of the trade and the freeing
of all slaves. It is interesting to note that the year 1787,
when Cugoano was calling publicly for abolition was the
same year the white abolitionist, Thomas Clarkson, and
others formed the Committee for Abolition of the African
Slave Trade. And all this was before William Wilberforce
became actively involved in the fight.

Cugoano's book, from which his comments will be
drawn, is entitled *Thoughts and Sentiments of the Evil and
Wicked Traffic of the Slavery and Commerce of the Human
Species*. The book, published in 1787, made him the first
published African critic of the transatlantic slave trade. In
the book, Cugoano responded to many arguments that
were being set out by the supporters of the slave trade and
put out fresh arguments of his own. Many of his arguments
are theological, that is, relating to his understanding of
who God is and how God works. Words and phrases like
"refined", "intricate" and "pulpit rhetoric" have been used
to describe his arguments and comments.[47] These arguments and comments on a whole range of issues will be
discussed in the following chapters. He tended to be more
trenchant and less diplomatic than his friend Equiano.
This is perhaps because whereas Equiano was the public
figure who went about the country speaking and rousing
the public behind the cause, Cugoano was essentially a
theologian. Whilst Equiano would have needed to keep as
many people on board as possible, Cugoano would tend
to follow through the logic of his argument, even if the
end result was not very comfortable for his readers. He
constantly argued that those involved in slavery would
meet an awful judgement from God,[48] and even though

he sent copies of this book to King George III and the Prince of Wales, he also argued that noble people and priest would bear a double load of guilt for supporting the trade.[49]

Concluding Remarks

These then are the short sketches of the lives of the four people that we will look at. Based on the stories, Sancho might be called "the Poet" because his letters were so beautifully crafted that the recipients kept them for many years. Gronniosaw, in our view, was remarkable for his poverty, but we will avoid calling him "Gronniosaw the Poor". Rather we will call him "Gronniosaw the Noble," because he was not only noble by birth, (as he was born to the nobility of north-eastern Nigeria), but noble in character (by staying with his former master's family long after his master had given him his freedom). Equiano might be called "the Activist". Although his writing, both in substance and style, has been given numerous commendations, it was his life and activities that gave his writing its credibility and force. It is also his high level of activities, his tour of the British isles campaigning for abolition, and even before then, his extensive travels while still a slave, that separate him from the other three. Cugoano, was easily the most radical in thinking of the four. His comments, as the reader will see, can be very direct. For example, he pointed out that slavery has a worse effect on slave holders than on the slaves themselves. "The slave-holders are meaner and baser than the African slaves, for while they subject and reduce [the slaves] to a degree with

brutes, they reduce themselves to a degree with devils".[50]
But Cugoano's radicalism was the result of unusual vision.
We have already seen the numerous things he saw well
ahead of his time, which have come to pass. So we will
call him "Cugoano the Visionary".

Chapter 3:
Attitude to Christianity

Introduction

It is often possible from reading somebody's life story or other writings to tell whether they are religious or not. For a Christian, very obvious clues would be references to such events as attending church or reading the Bible. They may even refer to particular church events relating to them, like their baptism. Beyond actual events, the kind of issues they bring up in their story could give an indication. They could, for example, make frequent references to God, Jesus Christ, salvation, heaven or other themes within Christianity. On the other hand, it might not be so much what subject they raise that suggests a Christian faith but how they treat the subject and what attitude can be perceived behind the text. In this chapter, we will look at the life stories of Gronniosaw and Equiano, the letters of Sancho and Cugoano's writing on the slave trade for

evidence of Christian faith and for their understanding
of the Christian religion.

Sancho the Poet

The first person we will be looking at is Ignatius Sancho.
Sancho the artistic writer, who became part of the London
literati, was also a keen church man. His letters show that he
went to church regularly. In one letter he teased himself for
going to church twice in one day and went on to describe the
two sermons. "Go to! – the man who visits church twice in
one day, must either be religious – curious – or idle – which-
ever you please, my dear friend – turn it the way which best
likes you – I will cheerily subscribe to it".[51] In other words,
you would probably think going to church twice in one day
is too religious, unnecessarily curious or simply idle, but
Sancho hereby confesses to it. He then went on to describe
the morning sermon by the minister, Harrison:

> By the way, Harrison was inspired this morning
> – his text was from Romans – chapter the –verse the
> – both forgot; - but the subject was to present heart,
> mind, soul, and all the affections – a living sacrifice
> to God; - he was most gloriously animated, and
> seemed to have imbibed the very spirit and manners
> of the great apostle.[52]

Then he described the afternoon sermon by a guest
minister:

> Our afternoon orator was a stranger to me – he was
> blest with a good, clear and well-toned articulate

voice; he preached from the Psalms – and took great pains to prove that God knew more than we… that a man in Westminster was totally ignorant of what was going forward in Whitechapel - that we might have some memory of what we did last week – but have no sort of conjecture of what we shall do tomorrow.[53]

In another letter, he comments not only on Harrison but on another minister, Dodd. Harrison, he writes, reads prayers well, there is a "dignity of expression in his psalms" and his "Litany" is so animated that it "almost carries the heart to the gates of heaven". Sancho avoids comparing Harrison with Dodd, as, in his view, this would be unfair, but notes that, "if Harrison reads prayers, and Dodd preaches at the same church – I should suppose greater perfection would not be found in England".[54] So committed to the church was Sancho that when Dodd was later charged with forgery and fraud, he wrote an open letter to the newspaper, *Morning Post*, to beg for Dodd. "I am one of the many who have been often edified by the graceful eloquence and truly Christian doctrine of the unfortunate Dr Dodd… Mercy, the anchor of my hope, inclines me to wish he might meet with Royal clemency".[55]

Evidence that Sancho was a committed Christian can also be seen in the ease with which he quotes the Bible in his letters. In one letter he writes:

> Smoking my morning pipe, the friendly warmth of glorious planet the sun – the leniency of the air – the cheerful glow of the atmosphere – made me involuntarily cry, "Lord, what is man that thou in

thy mercy art so mindful of him! Or what the son of man, that thou in thy mercy art so mindful of him![56]

This reference to Ps 8:4 is one of a number of references to the Book of Psalms. In the same letter, he quotes Ps 139:14, "we are fearfully and wonderfully made". He also refers to the creation of human beings by the "Sacred Architect" in His image (i.e. Gen 1:27) by blowing into man's nostrils (Gen 2:7) and mankind's "cruel fall"[57] recorded in Gen 3.

Sancho's regard for the Bible shows in the number of times he recommends it to other people. In a letter to one Mr Soubise, he writes, "Before I conclude, let me, as your true friend recommend seriously to you to make yourself acquainted with your Bible – Believe me, the more you study the word of God, your peace and happiness will increase the more with it".[58] In another letter to a young man called Jack Wingrave, the son of Sancho's friend, who was in India at the time, Sancho gives the following advice: "Read your Bible - As day follows night, God's blessing follows virtue – honor and riches bring up the rear – and the end is peace".[59]

He included the Bible and *The Book of Common Prayer* to a list of books he recommended to young people to read:

> I recommend all young people, who do me the honour to ask my opinion – I recommend, if their stomachs are strong enough for such intellectual food – Dr Young's Night Thoughts - Paradise Lost – and all the Season; - which, with Nelson's Feasts

and Fasts – a Bible and Prayer Book - used for twenty years to make my travelling library.[60]

Sancho's letters show that he sees Christianity mainly as a source of good behaviour. A word that comes repeatedly when he is thinking about what a Christian should be like is "charity". In an earlier letter to the same young fellow, Jack Wingrave, Sancho writes:

> I am clear, every good affection, every sweet sensibility, every heart-felt joy – humanity, politeness, charity – all, all, are streams from that sacred spring; - so that to say you are good-tempered, honest, social… is only in fact saying you live according to your DIVINE MASTER'S rule, and are a Christian.[61]

So for Sancho, a good Christian should be a person of good character, good-tempered, honest, polite, peaceful and so on. In one letter, he described humility as "the test of Christianity"[62]; in another, after he accidentally lost a letter meant for a friend, he asks his friend for forgiveness "as good Christians ought"[63] and in another letter, he points out that to be happy "despite of one's fortune" shows one is a Christian.[64]

Christianity, however, does not stop at character. A good Christian should help other people, readily. In a letter to a friend, Sancho writes, "I am sure you possess the kind of soul, that Christian philanthropy, which wishes well – and, in the sense of scripture, breathes peace and good-will to all".[65] In another letter to a lady friend, Sancho comments on the challenges of bringing up children, then adds:

Well! But what's all this to you? – you are no mother. – True, my sincerely esteemed friend – but you are something as good – you are perhaps better – much better and wiser I am sure than many mothers I have seen. – You, who believe in the true essence of the gospel – who visit the sick, cover the naked, and withdraw not your ear from the unfortunate.[66]

Sancho thus demonstrates that for him the essence of the Christian gospel is the way people treat each other.

Sancho himself appears to possess many of the most valued Christian attributes. His letters show him to be a humble man. Although some of his comments can be attributed to the writing style of the time, there is probably substance behind his constant expression of humility. A typical opening to his letters is this one which he wrote to one Mrs Cocksedge:

Dear Madam
    It would be affronting your good nature to offer an excuse for the trouble I am going to give you…[67]

Such a remark was not restricted to the opening of letters. In ending one of his letters to his friend Mr Meheux, he writes:

…although I confess myself exceedingly cold, yet I have warmth enough to declare myself yours sincerely.[68]

I Sancho.

Once, a writer in America wrote to Sancho asking his permission to publish two letters Sancho had written to his friends which the man had found. The man's name was Edmund Rack, and he wrote, "I am so much pleased with these letters, on account of the humanity and strong good sense they contain, that I am very desirous of gaining thy permission to print them in a collection of *Letters of Friendship*".[69] Sancho replied, pointing out to the man that, in the first place, the letters were no longer his but now the property of the recipients:

> As to the letters in question, you know, Sir, they are not now mine, but the property of the parties they are addressed to. – If you have had their permission, and think the simple effusions of a poor Negro's heart worth mixing with better things, you have my free consent to do as you please with them.[70]

Sancho's constant blessing of his friends in his letters also suggest that he received a good measure of that peace which he had pointed out was God's gift to the Christian. In letter after letter, Sancho took time to proclaim blessings on the person he was addressing. In a letter to a young family friend, Sancho writes:

> May you live to be a credit to your great and good friends, and a blessing and comfort to your honest parents! – May you my child, pursue, through God's mercy, the right paths of humility, candour, temperance, benevolence – with an early piety, gratitude, and praise to [God].[71]

Writing about his week to a friend, Sancho adds this comment about how his wife helped out with the work:

> Mrs Sancho has had a blessed week of it…She was forced to break sugar and attend shop. – God bless her and reward her! – she is good – good in heart good in principle – good by habit – good by Heaven! God forgive me, I had almost sworn![72]

To another friend whose family had just had a baby Sancho writes:

> I have pleasure in congratulating you upon Mrs W's happy delivery and pleasing increase of her family; - it is the hope and wish of my heart, that your comforts in all things may multiply with your years – that in the certain great end – you may immerge without pain – full of hope – from corruptible pleasure - to immortal and incorruptible life – happiness without end – and past human comprehension.[73]

Reading through Sancho's letters, one is conscious that behind them was a devout Christian man. He not only went to church regularly but followed the fortunes of the ministers. In a letter to one Miss L, Sancho writes:

> As to Dr Dodd, the last I heard of him – was that he was in France; - he has not preached for these nine Sundays at Pimlico. – You did not tell me the name of your Suffolk preacher – I fancy it was Dr Wollaston – who is reckoned equal to Dodd; I am glad you have him.[74]

He used Bible verses effortlessly, interweaving them with his points. In one letter he even quotes the words of the General Confession of the Book of Common Prayer, "We have left undone those things we should have done".[75] He saw Christianity as the source of good character and charitable deeds and lived out this understanding by way of his own generosity. His letters show that he was not a rich man. He sometimes referred to himself as poor and appears to have depended on his friends for material support. But he was rich in heart and he generously allowed the content of his heart to flow into his letters. When he referred to his writing as "the simple effusions of a poor Negro's heart," this was out of his customary humility. In fact, this was an effusion of rich blessings probably born out of having a good measure of peace within himself; peace and generosity rooted in a secure relationship with God.

Gronniosaw the Noble

Gronniosaw was noble not only because he was the grandson of the king of Zaara, which is in the north east of present day Nigeria, but because he was noble in character, staying with his master's family long after he had got his freedom. His story also shows that he was a committed Christian. The preface to the story written by W Shirley, shows that the very reason the story was written was to put on record Gronniosaw's remarkable faith:

> This account of the life and spiritual experiences of James Albert [as Gronniosaw was called] was taken from his own mouth, and committed to paper by

the elegant pen of a young Lady of the town of
Leominster, for her private satisfaction, and without
any intention at first that it should be made public.
But now she has been prevailed on to commit it to
the press, as it is apprehended, this little history contains matter well worthy the notice and attention of
every Christian reader... How deeply it must affect
a tender heart, not only to be reduced to the last
extremity himself, but to have his wife and children
perishing for want before his eyes! Yet his faith did
not fail him; he put his trust in the Lord and he was
delivered. And at this instant, though born in an
exalted station of life, and now under the pressure
of various afflicting providences, I am persuaded
(for I know the man) he would rather embrace the
dunghill, having Christ in his heart, than give up
his spiritual possessions and enjoyment, to fill the
throne of princes.[76]

Gronniosaw's story shows him to be what is often
called a "contemplative". That is, somebody who is biased
towards experiencing God through prayer and reflection
moreso than through focusing on practical action. As
with most contemplatives, his natural disposition may
have inclined him towards that bias. His description of
his life in Africa before he was enslaved shows him to be
a thoughtful and reflective person:

I had, from my infancy, a curious turn of mind,
was more grave and reserved in my disposition than
either of my brothers and sisters. I often teased them
with questions they could not answer; for which

reason they disliked me, as they supposed that I was either foolish, or insane… I was frequently lost in wonder at the works of creation: was afraid, uneasy, and restless, but could not tell for what. I wanted to be informed of things that no person could tell me; and was always dissatisfied. These wonderful impressions begun in my childhood, and followed me continually till I left my parents…[77]

Much later in life, this contemplative disposition continued to manifest. In his story, Gronniosaw described how he used to go off to a tree near his master's house to spend time on his own:

About a quarter of a mile from my master's house, stood a large remarkably fine oak-tree, in the midst of a wood; I often used to be employed there in cutting down trees, (a work I was very fond of) and I seldom failed going to this place every day; sometimes twice a day if I could be spared. It was the highest pleasure I ever experienced to sit under this oak, for there I used to pour out my complaints before the Lord; and when I had any particular grievance, I needed to go there, and talk to the tree, and tell my sorrows as if it were to a friend.[78]

Here I often lamented my own wicked heart and undone state; and found more comfort and consolation than I ever was sensible of before. Whenever I was treated with ridicule and contempt, I used to come here and find peace.[79]

This lonely place offered him many opportunities to pray:

> ...as I was then quite alone [at the tree], and my heart lifted up to God, and I was enabled to pray continually; and blessed for ever be His holy name, He faithfully answered my prayers. I can never be thankful enough to Almighty God for the many comfortable opportunities I experienced there.[80]

Gronniosaw's gratitude for the opportunity to spend time with God rather than focusing entirely on practical help or deliverance received from God is significant in itself.

Gronniosaw's faith can be seen not only in the time he spent praying but in the space he gave to prayer in his story. At the time the story was written, he was about 60,[81] so he would have had 60, years worth of life events to relate to the readers. Added to this is the fact that his story is really short, running into only 30 pages – compared to Sancho's 159 letters, and the books of Equiano and Cugoano, each of which are about 150 pages. Yet he took time to record not only his own prayers but those of others. It could be judged that prayer was important to Gronniosaw by the number he included in his story. For example, regarding his first master, who was the captain of a Dutch ship, he writes: "I have since thought that he must have been a serious man. His actions corresponded very well with such a character. He used to read prayers in public to the ship's crew every Sabbath day".[82] Later on in his life, he was bought by a man called Mr Freelandhouse. "He took me home with him, and made me kneel down, and put my two hands together, and prayed for me, and every night and morning he did the same".[83]

More evidence of Gronniosaw's Christian faith can be seen in his frequent quotation of the Bible to support his points. He described how, at a time he was feeling very low, while still at the house of Mr Freelandhouse, he was helped by a Bible passage:

> The last night that I continued in this place [i.e. the tree], in the midst of my distress, these words were brought home upon my mind, *behold the Lamb of God*.[84] I was something comforted at this, and began to grow easier, and wished for day, that I might find these words in my bible.[85]

At another time of misery and doubts he was comforted by another scripture passage:

> The more I saw of the beauty and glory of God, the more I was humbled under a sense of my own vileness. I often repaired to my old place of prayer, and I seldom came away without consolation. One day this scripture was applied to my mind, *And ye are complete in Him, which is the head of all principalities and powers*.[86]

Gronniosaw saw this as God's way of raising his spirit when he was getting overwhelmed by his troubles, and he supports this belief with another Bible verse:

> The Lord was pleased to comfort me by the application of many gracious promises at times when I was ready to sink under my trouble. *Wherefore he is also*

able to save them to the uttermost that come into God by Him, seeing He ever liveth to make intercession for them. Heb x. 14. *For by one offering He hath perfected for ever them that are sanctified.*[87]

Much of what can be discerned of how Gronniosaw understood the Christian religion or what a Christian should be like appears strongly linked to his own life experiences. Going back to his description of his childhood experiences, the reader might recall his statement that from his childhood, he was afraid, even though he could not tell what for. It would appear that this fear stayed with him his whole life. He tended to associate Christianity with protection. It could be said that for Gronniosaw a Christian was first and foremost a person protected and provided for by God. He is a person that God fights for and whose enemies are automatically the enemies of God. His understanding of God will be discussed more fully in a later chapter. For now, let us consider two examples of God's protection/provision for him. The first was early in his life when he was almost killed by a king in Africa who thought he was a spy for the kingdom of Bornu (his birthplace). He described here the events on the day he was to be beheaded by the king:

> The morning I was to die, I was washed, and all my gold ornaments made bright and shinning, and then carried to the palace, where the king was to behead me himself (as is the custom of the place). He was seated upon a throne at the top of an exceeding large yard, or court, which you must go through to enter the palace; it is as wide and spacious as a

large field in England. I had a lane of lifeguards to
go through. I guessed it to be about three hundred
paces.

I was conducted by my friend the merchant,
about half way up; then he durst proceed no further: I went up to the king alone. I went with an
undaunted courage, and it pleased God to melt
the heart of the king, who sat with his cimeter in
his hand ready to behead me; yet, being himself so
affected, he dropped it out of his hand, and took
me upon his knees, and wept over me. I put my
right hand round his neck, and pressed him to my
heart.[88]

The factuality of this account has been doubted by
some writers. It does seem implausible that a king surrounded by palace courtiers would break down and sink
his head on the chest of a 15-year-old boy. But it is not
totally impossible. In any case, it is not crucial to our
point whether the story is true or not. The issue for us is
the insight it gives into Gronniosaw's ideas about God,
that is, his belief that this was God's handiwork.

The second intervention by God was when Gronniosaw
and his family were starving to death. At one point, they
were given four large carrots by a gardener and they ate
only one a day. They had nothing to make fire with, so
they could not boil the carrots. Gronniosaw himself did
not eat any of it out of concern for his family.

> We lived in this manner till our carrots were gone;
> then my wife began to lament because of our poor
> babes, but I comforted her all I could; still hoping

and believing, that my God would not let us die, but that it would please him to relieve us, which He did almost by a miracle.

We went to bed as usual, before it was quite dark, (as we had neither fire nor candle) but had not been there long, before some person knocked at the door and inquired if James Albert [as Gronniosaw was called] [repetition] lived there? I answered in the affirmative, and rose immediately. As soon as I opened the door, I found it was the servant of an eminent attorney who resided at Colchester. He asked me how it was with me? If I was almost starved? I burst out crying, and told him I was indeed. He said his master supposed so, and that he wanted to speak with me, and I must return with him.[89]

It turned out to be an attorney who Gronniosaw had known when Gronniosaw was working for somebody else. He told Gronniosaw that he had thought a great deal about him of late, he suspected that Gronniosaw was probably in great need, and he could not rest until he had sent somebody to inquire after him. He was "greatly affected" when he heard how much Gronniosaw had been suffering of late, gave him a guinea and promised to help him in the future.

I could not help exclaiming, O! the boundless mercies of my God! I prayed unto Him and He has heard me; I trusted in Him and He has preserved me; where shall I begin to praise Him, or how shall I love Him enough?[90]

There is much more evidence to give about Gronniosaw's Christian faith and much more to describe about his understanding of Christianity than has been done here. For example, he had a sense of his worthlessness as a human being before God, which was sometimes excruciating. He also had an expectation on the moral standard a Christian should live up to. These aspects will, however, be discussed in other chapters. The description of his idea of Christianity given here will suffice for now. Here was a deeply thoughtful fellow, who, upon conversion to Christianity, became a deeply reflective and prayerful Christian. He had a deep fear of the unknown which coupled with the disempowering nature of slavery would have made him extremely vulnerable. But he was not paralysed by this vulnerability. Rather he threw himself into God's hands, as he believed every Christian should. And he was convinced that time after time, God did come to his rescue.

Equiano the Activist

Equianio's story about his life gives much insight into what kind of a Christian he was and what he understood the Christian religion to be about. He was baptized in 1759 during the time he was staying with the Guerin sisters in London. This is how he described the events leading up to the baptism:

> While I was attending these ladies, their servants told me I could not go to Heaven unless I was baptised. This made me very uneasy, for I had now some faint idea of a future state. Accordingly, I com-

municated my anxiety to the eldest Miss Guerin, with whom I [had] become a favourite, and pressed her to have me baptised, when to my great joy she told me I should… I was baptised in St Margaret's church, Westminster, in February 1759, by my present name. The clergyman, at the same time, gave me a book called *A Guide to the Indians*, written by the Bishop of Sodor and Man.[91]

This book, which was a guide to the knowledge and practice of Christianity,[92] and the Bible, which he would later buy with his own money while working as a slave in the Caribbean, would become his two favourite books.

At one of our trips to St Kitt's I had eleven bits of my own; and my friendly captain lent me five bits more, with which I bought a Bible. I was very glad to get this book, which I scarcely could meet with any where. I think there was none sold in Montserrat… My Bible and the Guide to the Indians, the two books I loved above all the others…[93]

Equiano's use of Bible stories and quotations suggests that he did spend time reading the Bible. Take for example, this description of how slaves brought from Africa to America were sold at an auction:

On a signal given (as the beat of a drum) the buyers rush at once into the yard where the slaves are confined, and make a choice of that parcel they like best. The noise and clamour with which this is attended, and the eagerness visible in the countenances of the buyers, serve but a little to increase the apprehensions of the terrified Africans…. I remember in the vessel in which I was brought over, in the men's apartment, there were several brothers, who in the sale, were sold in different lots, and it was very moving on this occasion to see and hear their cries at parting. O, ye nominal Christian! Might not an African ask you, learned you this from your God, who says unto you, Do unto all men as you would men should do unto you? [94]

In this way he used Jesus's words in Mat 7:12 (also, Luk 6:31) often called the Golden Rule,[95] to challenge the countries behind the slave trade. He used another of Jesus's sayings to challenge white people who steal the very little possessions African slaves have and those who rape African women in the Caribbean. He began by describing how field-slaves use their time for rest or refreshment to collect grass which they tie in bundles and take to town or market to sell:

Nothing is more common than for the white people on this occasion to take the grass from them without paying for it; and not only so, but too often also, to my knowledge, our clerks, and many others, at the same time have committed acts of violence on the poor, wretched, and helpless females; whom I have seen for hours stand crying to no purpose, and get no redress or pay of any kind. Is not this one common and crying sin enough to bring down God's judgement on the islands? He tells us that oppressor and oppressed are both in his hands; and if these are not the poor, the broken-hearted, the

blind, the captive, the bruised, which our Saviour
speaks of, who are they?[96]

This is a reference to Luk 4:18-19 where Jesus said:

> The Spirit of the Lord is on me,
> because he has anointed me
> to preach good news to the poor.
> He has sent me to proclaim freedom for the pris-
> oners
> and recovery of sight for the blind,
> to release the oppressed,
> to proclaim the year of the Lord's favor.

It is noteworthy that this passage used by Equiano
over two hundred years ago has become very popular
among Christians fighting for poor and oppressed people
around the world. Another example of Equiano's use of
the Bible is when another black man complained to him
that his master had taken his fish. "Sometimes when a
white man takes away my fish, I go to my master, and he
get me my right; and when my master by strength take
away my fishes, what me must do?" the man asked him.
"This artless tale," Equiano writes, "moved me much,
and I could not help feeling that just cause Moses had in
redressing his brother against the Egyptian."[97] This is a
reference to Ex 2:11-12, which states:

> One day, after Moses had grown up, he went out
> to where his own people were and watched them
> at their hard labor. He saw an Egyptian beating a
> Hebrew, one of his own people. Glancing this way

and that and seeing no one, he killed the Egyptian and hid him in the sand.

Another important indication of Equiano's Christian faith is that God is always at the back of his mind. When things go well, he sees this as help from God. For example, the first time he met his long-term master, Michael Pascal, he saw this as the work of "the kind and unknown hand of the Creator."[98] Regarding the time he narrowly avoided being sold by his master he writes, "my soul glorified God,"[99] a reference to Luk 1:46 (the Magnificat). When things go wrong, his most commonresponse is to "look upon God." That was his advice to the poor fisherman whose master took his fish, and he himself had to do the same from time to time.

> I experienced many instances of ill usage, and have seen many injuries done to other negroes in our dealings with Europeans: and, amidst our recreations, when we have been dancing and merry-making, they, without cause, have molested and insulted us. Indeed I was more than once obliged to look upon God on high, as I had advised the poor fisherman some time before.[100]

The comment by Equiano to "look upon God" when maltreated by the powerful is a good indication of his understanding of what the Christian religion is all about. It is fair to say that for Equiano, his belief in the justice of God lies at the foundation of his understanding of Christianity. When he comments "look upon God" he means "look upon God to give you justice". He believed that since God is just, Christians, as children of God, should be just. This belief in the justice of God and the expectation that those who claim to be God's children should likewise be just runs through Equiano's story of his life. It formed the background to his question above, "O, ye nominal Christian! …learned you this from your God, who says unto you, Do unto all men as you would men should do unto you?" [101]

When Christians act in a cruel way, there is clear incredulity in the tone of Equiano's narrative. Take for example, this story of an African slave caught trying to escape:

> When I was in Montserrat I knew a negro man, named Emmanuel Sankey, who endeavoured to escape from his miserable bondage, by concealing himself on board of a London ship; but fate did not favour the poor oppressed man; for, being discovered when the vessel was under sail, he was delivered up again to his master. This *Christian master* immediately pinned the wretch down to the ground at each wrist and ankle, and then took some sticks of sealing wax, and lighted them, and dropped it all over his back.[102]

By putting "Christian master" in italics, Equiano highlights the contradiction between the man's actions and the faith he claims to be his.

Much the same understanding is evident in Equiano's newspaper articles which he often wrote in response to other articles or books supporting the slave trade. In a response to Mr Gordon Turnbull, who wrote in defence of the slave trade, Equiano writes:

> Can any man be a Christian who asserts that one part of the human race were ordained to be in perpetual bondage to another? Is such an assertion consistent with that spirit of meekness, of justice, of charity, and above all, that brotherly love which it enjoins?[103]

In another newspaper article in response to a clergy man, Rev Raymund Harris, who wrote a book arguing that the Bible supports slavery, Equiano writes:

> I could not have believed any man in your office would have dared to come forth in public in these our days to vindicate the accursed Slave Trade on any ground; but least of all by the law of Moses, and by that of Christ in the Gospel.[104]

This understanding also shows in his comments regarding politicians and governments. For example, in response to those who were comparing the plight of black slaves to those of poor white people, he quotes to them the law which put a price on the life of a black man:

> By the 329th Act, page 125, of the Assembly of Barbados, it is enacted, "That if any negro, or other slave, under punishment by his master, or his order, for running away, or any other crime or misdemeanour towards his said master, unfortunately shall suffer in life or member, no person whatsoever shall be liable to a fine; but if any man shall

out of *wantonness, or only of bloody-mindedness, or cruel intention, wilfully kill a negro, or other slave, of his own, he shall pay into the public treasury fifteen pounds sterling.*"[105]

This law, Equiano pointed out, is the same in other countries of the Caribbean and prompts him to ask: "do not the assembly which enacted it deserve the appellation of savages and brutes rather than of Christians and men?"[106]

Equiano did not apply this understanding only to other people, but to himself as well. He would not escape from his master even though he had opportunities to do so because he believed in doing everything and dealing with all people with honesty. For example, when he found himself back in the Caribbean, where slaves were treated very harshly, after he had enjoyed relative comfort in London, he writes:

> My mind was therefore hourly replete with inventions and thoughts of being freed, and, if possible, by honest and honourable means; for I always remembered the old adage; and I trust it has ever been my ruling principle, that honesty is the best policy; and likewise that other golden precept – to do unto all men as I would they should do unto me.[107]

On occasions when he met misfortune, he thought this was God's just punishment for some wrongdoing. This happened for example, when he suffered the disappointment of being sold to another master, whereas he was expecting to be soon freed.

> I wept bitterly for some time and began to think that I must have done something to displease the Lord, that he thus punished me so severely. This filled me with painful reflections on my past conduct: I recollected that on the morning of our arrival at Deptford, I had rashly sworn that as soon as we reached London I would spend the day in rambling and sport. My conscience smote me for this unguarded expression: I felt that the Lord was able to disappoint me in all things, and immediately considered my present situation as a judgement of Heaven on account of my presumptuous swearing.[108]

So it could be deduced from all this that Olaudah Equiano was a good Christian man. Unlike Sancho, whose faith is shown out in his elegantly composed letters, written mostly from his grocery shop at Charles Street in central London, or Gronniosaw, whose story is told as a reflection on a series of spiritual experiences, Equiano's faith emerges out of the rough and tumble of sailing on the high seas from one continent to another, being sold from master to master, working hard to make money on the side and so on. He had to save up for a Bible, and from his quotations, appears to have made very good use of the book. Reading through his accounts one can see why his story struck a cord with the British public immediately when it was published. As regards his understanding of Christianity, what comes out is a man for whom the justice of God is the very foundation. Since God is just, Christians, God's children, must be just. If not, then they are simply making bogus claims.

Cugoano the Visionary

Cugoano, the last of the four characters, was the youngest and the most strident in his remarks. He was also a baptised Christian. This is how he described the events leading to his baptism:

> When I was kidnapped and brought away from Africa, I was about 13 years of age, in the year of the Christian era 1770; and after being about nine or ten months in the slave-gang at Grenada, and about one year at different places in the West Indies, with Alexander Campbell, Esq.; who brought me to England in the end of the year 1772, I was advised by some people to get myself baptised, that I might not be carried away and sold again.[109]

Cugoano's book contains many references from the Bible. In fact, it contains more Biblical references than the work of all the other three African writers put together. But this is mainly because unlike the other books, Cugoano's *Thoughts and Sentiments* is a criticism from a Christian point of view of the slave trade. For example, he writes:

> ...as we have been robbed our natural rights as men, and treated as beasts, those who have injured us, are like to them who have robbed the widow, the orphan, the poor and the needy of their right and

whose children are rioting on the spoils of those who are begging at their doors for bread.[110]

Cugoano draws on two Biblical images here. The first is Deut 27:19, "cursed is the man who withholds justice from the alien, the fatherless or the widow." The second is Jesus's story about the rich man and Lazarus (Luk 16:19-31). In both cases the oppressors met with grave consequences.

In another reference, he used the Biblical story of King David and his offence against Uriah to describe the responsibility of those in authority. Uriah was a soldier in the Israelite army, while David was king. King David wanted to take Uriah's wife so he directed Uriah's commanding officer in the army to take Uriah to the war front and withdraw without him so he would be killed by the enemy. After this plan was carried out, and Uriah was killed by Israel's enemy, the Ammonites, God was not in doubt who was responsible and sent Nathan the Prophet to David with these words, "You struck down Uriah the Hittite with the sword and took his wife to be your own. You killed him with the sword of the Ammonites. Now, therefore the sword will never depart from your house." (2 Sam 11:8-10) Cugoano believed that highly placed people in Britain were similarly responsible for what was going on in the country. This is particularly so for kings:

> For kings are the ministers of God, to do justice, and not to bear the sword in vain, but to revenge wrath upon them that do evil. But if they do not in such a case as this, the cruel oppression of thousands, and the blood of the murdered Africans who are slain

by the sword of cruel avarice, must rest upon their own guilty heads in as eventually and plain a sense as it was David that murdered Uriah.[111]

Among many references he likened black people's plea for justice to that of Mordercai who used to go to king Xerxes' gate in sackcloth and ashes to plead for his people (Es 4);[112] he asked in respect for the end of slave trade, "Does not wisdom cry?" a reference to Prov 8:1; and he quoted Equiano's favourite commandment, "do to other as you would they do to you" to make the point that the slave-holders would not like to receive the same treatment they gave out – to be enslaved, treated like dogs and sold like animals.[113]

Cugoano also employed the Bible to defend the idea of punishment for those who make slaves of others. He does this by reminding the reader of the story of Saul and Agag the king of the Amalekites (1 Sam 15). As a punishment for Agag's sins, God had commanded Saul to attack the Amalekites and to kill all the inhabitants of the land. But Saul spared Agag. This disobedience made God angry, so he decided to remove Saul as king. Based on this Cugoano writes:

> All our Amalekite sins, and even the chief and darling of them, the avaricious and covetous Agags, should be cut off for ever. But if we spare them, and leave them to remain alive in stubborn disobedience to the law and commandments of God, we should in that case, be like Saul, cut off ourselves from the kingdom of his grace.[114]

Cugoano did not use the Bible only when he was supporting his case, but also challenged those who were using the Bible to justify the slave trade. For example, he challenged those who said that Moses started slavery. He pointed out that, in the first place, some of the men putting forward such arguments did not believe in the scriptures, anyway. They only referred to the bits which suited their purpose[115] and their usage was inconsistent and dialogistical.[116] It must be a perverted use of the Bible, he argued, because they were using it as a precedent to commit wickedness.[117]

Cugoano's commitment to Christianity also shows in his interest in Christian education. When he was making proposals regarding abolition, one of his ideas was that while arrangements were being made to free all slaves, slave-holders should be required to arrange Christian education for the slaves in their care:

> And that they should not hinder, but cause and procure some suitable means of instruction for them [i.e. the slaves] in the knowledge of the Christian religion… that by no means, under any pretence whatsoever, either for themselves or their masters, the slaves under their subjection should not be suffered to work on the Sabbath days.[118]

He also longed for the day when some Christians could be sent to Africa to teach them Christianity:

> …it is my highest wish and earnest prayer to God, that some encouragement could be given to send [to Africa] able school masters, and intelligent min-

isters, who would be faithful and able to teach the Christian religion. This would be doing great good to the Africans, and be a kind restitution for the great injuries that they have suffered.[119]

His book *Thoughts and Sentiments* he had written because he wanted to instruct other black people in the things of Christianity. He also had the intention of opening a school to instruct other black people on the Christian religion.[120]

Cugoano's book, *Thoughts and Sentiments*, suggests that he sees the Christian religion, at least in part, as a set of principles for organising society – principles based on God's laws. This is an impression that persists even after considering that *Thoughts and Sentiments*, our main source for his ideas, was written as a criticism of the slave trade. In page after page of the book, Cugoano points out that slavery runs against what one would expect in a Christian country, against the principles of a Christian civilisation. He looked at it from the point of view of love, "The whole law of God is founded upon love, and the two grand branches of it are these: Thou shalt love the Lord thy God with all thy heart and with all thy soul; and though shalt love thy neighbour as thyself."[121]

This kind of love, Cugoano explains, was what God intended from the beginning when human beings were created:

> ...they were created male and female, and pronounced to be in the image of God, and, as his representatives, to have dominion over the lower creation: and their Maker, who is love, and the

intellectual Father of Spirits, blessed them, and
commanded them to arise in a bond of union of
nature and of blood, each being a brother and a
sister together, and each the lover and the loved of
one another.[122]

The Devil, however, stepped in and thwarted God's
plans and some human beings started to follow the Devil's
ways:

But when they were envied and invaded by the
grand enslaver of men [i.e. the Devil], all their jar-
ring incoherency arose, and those who adhered to
their pernicious usurper soon became envious, hate-
ful, and started hating each other. And those who
go on to injure, ensnare, oppress, and enslave their
fellow creatures, manifest their hatred to men, and
maintain their own infamous dignity and vassalage,
as servants of sin and the Devil.[123]

True civilisation, for Cugoano, is carried forth by
those operating on the original plan of God, based on
love. Europe, in allowing slavery to take place, had abandoned the right principles for nation building. "The several nations of Europe that have joined in that iniquitous traffic of buying, selling and enslaving men, must
in course have left their own laws of civilisation to adopt
those of barbarians and robbers."[124]

Specifically regarding Britain, he writes:

In a Christian era, in a land where Christianity is
planted, where every one might expect to behold the
flourishing growth of every virtue, extending their

harmonious branches with universal philanthropy wherever they came; but, on the contrary, almost nothing else is to be seen abroad but the bramble of ruffians, barbarians and slave-holders, grown up to a powerful luxuriance in wickedness.[125]

Hence, he goes on to suggest that these people who act in ways that are totally contrary to what he understands as Christian should not be called so:

I cannot but wish, for the honor of Christianity, that the bramble grown up amongst them, was known to the heathen nations by a different name, for sure the depredators, robbers and ensnarers of men can never be Christians, but ought to be held as the abhorrence of all men, and the abomination of all mankind, whether Christians or heathens.[126]

This brings us to another key part of Cugoano's understanding of Christianity, namely, that it is about what you do and how you live and not about an intense church life:

Why think ye prayers in churches and chapels only will do ye good, if your charity does not extend to pity and regard your fellow creatures perishing through ignorance, under the heavy yoke of subjection and bondage, to the cruel and avaricious oppression of brutish profligate men, and when both the injured, and their oppressors, dwell in such a vicinity as equally to claim your regard?[127]

In one long, telling passage, Cugoano describes what slaves go through from when they are captured to when they are sold and showed his incredulity that those who do this call themselves Christians:

> The treacherous, perfidious and cruel methods made use of in procuring them, are horrible and shocking. The bringing them to the ship and factories, and subjecting them to brutal examinations, stripped naked and markings, is barbarous and base. The stowing them in the holds of the ships like goods of burden, with closeness and stench, is deplorable… when they arrive at the destined port in the colonies, they are again stripped naked for the brutal examination of their purchasers to view them… friends and near neighbours must be parted never to meet again… daughters are clinging to their mothers, and mothers to daughters… fathers, mothers, and children, locked in each others arms, are begging never to be separated… the husband will be pleading for his wife, and the wife praying for her children… and some will be still weeping for their native shore, and their dear relatives and friends, and other enduring connections which they left behind… And when sold and delivered up to their inhuman purchasers, a more heart-piercing scene cannot well take place… should any of them still linger and not part as readily as the their owners would have them, the flogger is called on, and they are soon drove away with the bloody commiseration of the cutting fangs of the whip lashing their naked bodies… Alas! Alas! Poor unhappy mortals!

To experience such treatment from men that take upon themselves the sacred name of Christians![128]

Hence, it could be concluded that the evidence shows that Ottobah Cugoano was a baptised Christian. Because he did not write much about himself in his book *Thoughts and Sentiments*, little else is known about his church life. It is obvious, however, from the way he used the Bible that he was a devout Christian man. In his attack against the slave trade, he not only drew on the Bible to support his case, but was knowledgeable enough to refute the case of his opponents with the Bible. His understanding of Christianity, as can be discerned from his book, is of a system of principles for running society which is based on the law of God. In a similar way, he is critical of those who present themselves as Christians but do nothing in the face of the oppression of the poor and defenceless around them. To be a Christian is to act like one.

Concluding Remarks

It is clear from the above that Sancho, Gronniosaw, Equiano and Cugoano were four Africans whose writing showed different understandings of Christianity. But as has already been stated, the nature of their understanding is related to their circumstances and the purpose of their books from which their beliefs have been derived. For example, Sancho's book, *Letters*, from which a picture of his views was built, is a collection of letters he wrote to friends, so it is understandable that Christianity for him boils down to the source of good character. Similarly, Cugoano's book, *Thoughts and Sentiments*, was written as a criticism of the slave trade and the countries engaged in it, so the understanding of Christianity that would emerge from him was always likely to be about the principles of good society.

Secondly, the four people were from different generations. For example, 1770, the year Gronniosaw's book was published, at which time he was already over sixty, was the same year Cugoano was kidnapped and sold into slavery as a boy of thirteen. This generational gap also meant that they lived during different eras in Britain. Sancho and Gronniosaw lived in Britain before the abolition movement gathered pace; whereas Equiano and Cugoano were in the prime of their life at that time.

All this means that a comparison of their views with each other has to be avoided. Instead, Sancho's example when he was describing two ministers at his church, Dodd and Harrison, will be followed. He imagined them working together, "...if Harrison reads prayers, and Dodd preaches at the same church – I should suppose greater perfection would not be found in England."[129]

Let us imagine that the different understandings of the four persons were put together. If for instance, Sancho, Gronniosaw, Equiano and Cugoano were asked to make a joint presentation, let us imagine how their joint presentation might be.

Sancho, if he starts, would probably begin by explaining how Christianity is the best source of good personal character. He would mention such qualities as gentleness, politeness, honesty and generosity as the signs of a good Christian. These are the kind of qualities that Paul called "fruits of the Spirit" in Gal 5:22-23 – "love, joy, peace, patience, kindness, goodness, faithfulness, gentleness and self-control." Gronniosaw, if he follows, would probably stress the personal, spiritual dimensions of Christianity. He would try to make the audience aware of the many dangers lurking around in the world unseen by the naked eyes – dangers which should make people afraid. But thanks to God, who good Christians can always trust to help, there is protection against every kind of harm. He would encourage people to spend more time in prayer to be close to this God.

Equiano would move the presentation from the personal dimension to the corporate dimension. He would point out that at the very heart of Christianity is the way people treat each other. Christianity is nothing, if it is not about being just to other people. He would explain that because God is just, all who claim to follow him should be just. He may end by urging the audience that in order to be just they should adopt the Golden Rule, "Do to others as you would have them do to you" (Matt 7:12). Equiano's move from the personal to the corporate dimension would be taken a step further by Cugoano in the last presentation. He would point out the expectation that is made of a person who claims to be a Christian and of a country that claims to be a Christian country. He would tell them that Christianity is about the principles for building a good, progressive society. It places a responsibility on all the members of that society, although those who have important offices shoulder more of that responsibility. He would close by warning that collective judgement and punishment would follow any group of people or country that fails to measure up to those responsibilities.

CHAPTER 4:

UNDERSTANDING OF GOD

Introduction

Most people have their own particular understanding of who God is. Even people who do not believe in God or that God exists, have their own concept of God which they are then rejecting. Among Christians, a careful exploration would show different concepts of God. For example, some might see God mainly in terms of a loving, father-figure who is always willing to forgive and ever willing to include people in His kingdom, whereas some others might see God, primarily, as an upright, fair arbiter who abhors injustice and would punish wrongdoing wherever it has occurred. For Christians, the view they have of God affects other aspects of their Christian belief. Theology, the science of religious belief, in fact, literally means "the study of God" (i.e. *theo* = God, *logia* = study).

In the previous chapter, we looked at how Sancho, Gronniosaw, Equiano and Cugoano practiced the Christian faith and what was their understanding of Christianity. At the bottom of that understanding is the belief about God. In this chapter, we will examine their writing to glean out from them what each one of them believed about God. The obvious way to do this would be to look at their references to God and decide what, collectively, those references portray God as. We should also go behind obvious references and discern through what they write on other subjects or their behaviour what understanding of God is operating in their mind. We would like to reiterate that this work is, inevitably, limited by the material we have available.

Sancho the Poet

What we have from Sancho are letters he wrote to friends and acquaintances. We cannot, therefore, expect to find clear statements about the nature of God in his work, as though he was writing a theological book. What we can do, though, is to look for a pattern of comments about God in his letters. Some of the comments would be short or expressed in an off-handed way. The important question is which ideas about God appear repeatedly. What is given below is a mere sample from over 150 letters.

Taken as a whole, Sancho's letters show that he saw God, primarily, as a giver of good things. Describing his life in a letter to a friend he writes:

> The first part of my life was rather unlucky, as I was
> placed in a family who judged ignorance the best

and only security for obedience. – A little reading
and writing I got by unwearied application. – The
latter part of my life has been – thro' God's blessing,
truly fortunate, having spent it in the service of one
of the best families in the kingdom.[130]

In other words, his improved circumstance was a gift
from God. In another letter to a young family friend
spending time in Asia, Mr Jack Wingrave, Sancho writes,
"May the God of truth and fountain of all good enrich thy
heart and head with his spirit and wisdom – crown your
labours with success – and guard you from avarice."[131]

In several letters, he showed that he saw God as the
giver of good health. In the same letter to Mr Wingrave,
he writes, "You are greatly fortunate in enjoying your
health – for which I doubt not but you are truly thankful to the Almighty Giver".[132] He often thanked God for
his own health and the health of his family. In one letter
he adds this postscript about the health of his daughter,
Lydia, "We are in great hopes about poor Lydia – An honest and ingenious motherly woman in our neighbourhood
has undertaken the perfect cure of her – and we have
every reason to think, with God's blessing, she will."[133]
In another letter he writes, "Mrs Sancho remains, thank
God, very well – and all the rest ditto." Sancho, himself,
suffered from gout and often wrote about that:

> As soon as we can get a bit of house, we shall begin
> to look sharply for a bit of bread – I have strong
> hope – the more children, the more blessings – and
> if it pleases the Almighty to spare me from the

gout, I verily think the happiest part of my life is to come.[134]

In a letter to his friend, Mr Meheux, Sancho promised to write him again "if God, gout, and weather permit".[135]

Sancho saw God not only as a provider but a protector. Hence, in one letter he prays for his friends, "God bless them! feasting or fasting - sleeping or waking! - may God's providence watch over and protect them – and all such!"[136] and in another he urges the recipient: "Trust, trust in the Almighty – his providence is your shield – 'tis his love, 'tis his mercy, which has hitherto supported and kept you up."[137] Indeed, a key aspect of Sancho's understanding of God is that a God that provides and protects is trustworthy. Reacting to the death of a friend, the Duchess of Queensbury, Sancho writes:

> It was on Friday night, between ten and eleven, just preparing for my concluding pipe – the Duke of *Montagu*'s man knocks – "Have you heard the bad news?" – No   "The Duchess of Queensbury died last night" – I felt fifty different sensations – unbelief was uppermost... It is too true that the Almighty has called to her rich reward – she who, whilst on earth, approved herself his best delegate. – How blind, how silly, is the mortal who places any trust or hope in aught but the Almighty![138]

Sancho's point is that the transient nature of earthly life should tell anybody that only God, who has power beyond the grave, is worth relying on. Not even a duchess, with all her fame and fortune, can escape being reduced to nothing by death. One moment she was alive, the next moment she was dead. He writes:

> The day after you left town her Grace her grace died – that day week she was at my door – the day after I had the honor of a long audience in her dressing room – Alas! this hour blessed with health – crowned with honors – loaded with riches, and encircled with friends – the next reduced to a lump of poor clay – a tenement for worms.[139]

We can also see the same attitude to God from the way Sancho treated his material poverty. In a letter to one Mr Kisby, Sancho writes:

> More and more convinced of the futility of all our eagerness after worldly riches, my prayer and hope is only for bread, and to be enabled to pay what I owe. – I labour up hill against many difficulties – but God's goodness is my support – and his word my trust.[140]

On the same subject of poverty, he writes to a friend facing hard times, trying to comfort him with his own hardship. He points out how at the present moment he himself was "not quite worth ten shillings":

> One dawn of hope I enjoy from the old saw – that "gloomy beginnings are for the most part blessed with bright endings:" – may it be so with you, my friend! – At the worst you can only face about - and your lodgings and old friends will cordially receive

you – For my part, I have use for every mite of my philosophy – my state at present is that of suspense – God's will be done.[141]

Some could see this as fatalism (i.e., the belief that all events are predetermined and inevitable). For Sancho, though, the issue was a total trust in God and a belief that God's will, however it unfolds, would be for the best.

Sancho's belief that God was a giver of good things can be seen not only in the words he uses when he blesses people, but in his readiness to bless. It was as though he believed all he needed to do was proclaim a blessing and God would carry it out. In a letter to his friend Mr Meheux, thanking him, probably, for something he had written, Sancho writes:

> Go on, my honest heart, go on! – hold up the mirror to an effeminate gallimawfry [i.e. assortment]… Thou, my worthy Meheux, continue thy improvements; and may the Almighty bless thee with the humble mien of piety and content![142]

Regarding some young family friends who are soon to marry, he writes, "Is my sweet Polly married yet? Has she made Mr H happy? May they both enjoy every comfort God Almighty blesses his children with!"[143]

Sancho's preparedness to bless can be seen in this reply to a letter from one Mr Browne. After thanking him for his letter, Sancho writes:

> May you live to be a credit to your great and good friends, and a blessing and comfort to your honest parents! – May you my child, pursue, through

God's mercy, the right paths of humility, candour,
temperance, benevolence – with an early piety, gratitude, and praise to [God].[144]

The final aspect of Sancho's understanding of God
we want to deal with is his view that God rewards good
behaviour. He believed that a good Christian should
walk right with God, living according to God's laws, and
that in return God will bless that person with wellbeing.
Hence, as we saw in the previous section, he writes:

> I am clear, every good affection, every sweet sen-
> sibility, every heart-felt joy – humanity, polite-
> ness, charity – all, all, are streams from that sacred
> spring; - so that to say you are good-tempered, hon-
> est, social…is only in fact saying you live accord-
> ing to your DIVINE MASTER'S rule, and are a
> Christian.[145]

Such right living, God will reward, as he reflects here
in regard of a gift he received from one Mr Spinks, "I
wish I knew which way to shew my gratitude – The only
method I can think of, is to enjoy the benefits with a
thankful heart, and leave God in his own good time
to reward you."[146] To young Jack Wingrave he writes,
"Continue in right thinking, you will of course act well;
in well doing, you will insure the favor of GOD, and
the love of your friends, amongst whom pray reckon."[147]
He echoes the same sentiments in another letter to Jack
Wingrave, ten years later. He advises the young man.
"Read your Bible - As day follows night, God's blessing

follows virtue – honor and riches bring up the rear – and
the end is peace."[148]

A study of Sancho's comments about God in his letters, from which we have only given a few above, shows
that Sancho saw God as a kind of Providential Carer – the
giver of good things. Right from his early life, God's care
can be seen enabling him to get some education, thwart-
ing the ploys of the family that wanted to keep him illiter-
ate and ignorant. God's care extends to health, as Sancho
can be seen in his letters either pleading or thanking God
for the health of himself or that of other people. God's
providential care also meant he would sometimes protect people. Because God provides and protects, God is
trustworthy. Finally, Sancho believed that even though
God liked to give generously, God was not indifferent to
people's behavior. Rather, God was likely to reward good
behavior with even more blessings.

Gronniosaw the Noble

Gronniosaw's story shows that he saw God primarily as a
protector. He described at least two occasions when God
pulled him out from the jaws of death. These occasions
were described in the previous chapter and so will only be
referred to briefly. The first is when he was to be beheaded
by a king who thought he was a spy for the African kingdom of Bornu. God intervened and the king changed his
mind, dramatically, and spared his life.

> I was conducted by my friend the merchant, about
> half way up; then he durst proceed no further: I
> went up to the king alone. I went with an undaunted

courage, and it pleased God to melt the heart of the king, who sat with his cimeter in his hand ready to behead me; yet, being himself so affected, he dropped it out of his hand, and took me upon his knees, and wept over me.[149]

Gronniosaw's statement, "it pleased God to melt the heart of the king", shows who he believes is responsible for this strange turn of events.

The second event he recorded where God was clearly protecting him from complete demise was when he was helped by a certain man from Colchester. He and his family were slowly starving to death when one day, out of the blue, there was a knock on the door. It turned out to be the messenger of a man Gronniosaw had known sometime in the past. The man, who lived in Colchester, had asked his messenger to go and find Gronniosaw wherever he was, because he suspected that Gronniosaw was facing hard times and could not have peace until he had found Gronniosaw.

> This gentleman's name was Danniel, he was a sincere good Christian. He used to stand and talk with me frequently, when I worked on the road for Mr Hardbarar, and would have employed me himself, if I had wanted work. When I came to his house, he told me that he had thought a great deal about me of late, and was apprehensive that I must be in want, and could not be satisfied till he had sent to inquire after me. I made known my distress to him, at which he was greatly affected, and generously gave me a guinea, and promised to be kind to me in

future. I could not help exclaiming, *O the boundless mercies of my GOD!* [150]

Gronniosaw's gratitude continued after he used the guinea to buy the things they needed at home:

> I went immediately and bought some bread and cheese, and coal, and carried it home. My dear wife was rejoiced to see me return with something to eat. She instantly got up and dressed our babes, while I made a fire, and the first nobility in the land never made a better meal. We did not forget to thank the Lord for all his goodness to us.[151]

A curious aspect of Gronniosaw's story is the way he tends to portray whoever is his master in very good light. His description of his sale to his first master, the captain of a Dutch ship, showed that he believed the Dutch man actually saved him from death. This happened after he was spared from being beheaded in the Gold Coast (present day Ghana) after he had been taken there from Bornu (north east of present day Nigeria). Although the king did not kill him, he had ordered that Gronniosaw should not be allowed to return to Bornu, his home country, but should be sold into slavery.[152] But the appointed merchant and his partner had difficulty finding a buyer for Gronniosaw and got to the point where they were now considering killing him off.

> The next day he took me on board a French brig; but the captain did not choose to buy me; he said I was too small; so the merchant took me home with him again.

The partner, whom I have already spoken of as my enemy, was very angry to see me return, and again proposed putting an end to my life; for he represented to the other, that I should bring them into trouble and difficulties, and that I was so little that no person would buy me.

The merchant's resolution began to waver; and I was indeed afraid that I should be put to death: but however, he said he would try me once more.

A few days after a Dutch ship came into the harbour, and they carried me on board, in hopes that the captain would purchase me. As they went, I heard them agree, that if they could not sell me *then*, they would throw me overboard. I was in extreme agony when I heard this; and as soon as ever I saw the Dutch captain, I ran to him, and put my arms round him, and said, "Father, save me," (For I knew that if he did not buy me, I should be treated very ill, or possibly murdered.) And though he did not understand my language, yet it pleased the Almighty to influence him in my behalf and he bought me *for two yards of check*, which is of more value *there*, than in England.

Equally, Gronniosaw saw his second master as a good man, as he recalls here:

My master's ship was bound for Barbados. When we came there, he thought fit to speak of me to several gentlemen of his acquaintance, and one of them expressed a particular desire to see me. He had a great mind to buy me; but the Captain could not immediately be prevailed on to part with me; but however, as the gentleman seemed very solicitous, he at length let me go, and I was sold for 50 dollars (four and sixpenny pieces in English). My new master's name was Vanhorn, a young gentleman; his home was in New-England, in the city of New York, to which place he took me with him. He dressed me in his livery, and was very good to me.

Vanhorn sold Gronniosaw to another man, Mr Freelandhouse, who would later give Gronniosaw his freedom as he was dying: Freelandhouse was an acquaintance of Vanhorn. In Gronniosaw's words, he was:

> ...a very gracious, good Minister... he took a great deal of notice of me, and desired my master to part with me to him. He would not hear of it at first, but being greatly persuaded, he let me go, and Mr Freelandhouse gave 50 pound for me. – He took me home with him, and made me kneel down, and put my two hands together, and prayed for me, and every night and morning he did the same.[133]

Gronniosaw appears to think that this supply of "good" masters was God's handiwork. He seems to believe that God was protecting him by putting him in the care of men who liked him and looked after him.

Another important aspect of how Gronniosaw saw God is God's power. He believed that God could perform any miracle no matter how small or how big. This was why he was confident in the face of adversity. He gave

this description of one occasion when he lost his job with
a man called Mr Handbarar:

> We went on very comfortably all summer. We lived
> in a little cottage near Mr Handbarar's house; but
> when the winter came on I was discharged, as he
> had no further occasion for me. And now the pros-
> pect began to darken upon us again. We thought it
> most advisable to move our habitation a little nearer
> to the town, as the house we lived in was very cold,
> and wet, and ready to tumble down.
>
> The boundless goodness of God to me, has been
> so very great, that with the most humble gratitude
> I desire to prostrate myself before him; for I have
> been wonderfully supported in every affliction. My
> God never left me, I perceived light still thro' the
> thickest darkness.[154]

These are, obviously, words said in reflection much
later. But they are also meant to capture his feeling at the
time. Another example was when he and his family were
about to be thrown out of their lodging by the landlady.
They were behind both in rent and the cost of hiring a
loom which Gronniosaw's wife normally used to make
money, mainly because there children had fallen ill with
small pox and required all they had to keep them alive.
"Our three poor children fell ill of the small pox, this was
a great trial to us, but still I was persuaded in myself we
should not be forsaken."[155] Gronniosaw's plea to pay off
his debt as soon as his children got better fell on deaf ears.
It was either out with the rent or out on the street!

The apprehension of this plunged me into the deepest distress, considering the situation of my poor babes if they had been in health, I should have been less sensible of this misfortune. But my God *still faithful to his promise*, raised me a friend: Mr. Henry Gardney, a quaker; a gracious gentleman, heard of our distress, and sent a servant of his own to the woman we hired our room of, paid our rent, and bought all the goods, with my wife's loom, and gave it us all.[156]

The final aspect of Gronniosaw's understanding of God to look at is that of God as a spiritual being. Gronniosaw, perhaps more than all the others, saw God as a being acting outside the physical realm. This can be seen first in his language, such as in this reference to Col 2:10:

The more I saw of the beauty and glory of God, the more I was humbled under a sense of my own vileness. I often repaired to my old place of prayer, and I seldom came away without consolation. One day this scripture was applied to my mind, *And ye are complete in Him, which is the head of all principalities and powers.*[157]

The key phrase here is "principalities and powers" which makes the point that God (in Christ) not only has authority over secular powers of the world but, also, over unseen divinities.

This view of God which he had was reinforced by some strange experiences. He recalls one, which hap-

pened to him one day at the woods, where he often went
to pray:

> I was one day in a most delightful frame of mind,
> my heart so overflowed with love and gratitude to
> the author of all my comforts. – I was so drawn out
> of myself, and so filled and awed by the presence
> of God, I saw (or thought I saw) light inexpressibly
> dart down from heaven upon me, and shine around
> me for the space of a minute. I continued on my
> knees, and joy unspeakable took possession of my
> soul. The peace and serenity which filled my mind
> after this, was wonderful, and cannot be told. I
> would not have changed the situation, or being any
> one but myself for the world. I blessed God for my
> poverty, that I had no worldly riches or grandeur to
> draw my heart from him. I wished at that time if it
> had been possible for me to have continued on that
> spot for ever.[158]

It is because Gronniosaw saw God in his spiritual
aspect that he emphasizes the miraculous. Sometimes,
he goes beyond that to point out some mysterious hap-
penings. Two of these concerned people who treated
Gronniosaw badly, who in time met with misfortune. The
first was an acquaintance of the Freelandhouse family and
it happened when the family had all died and Gronniosaw
was on his own:

> About this time a young gentleman that was a par-
> ticular acquaintance of one of my young masters,
> pretended to be a friend to me, and promised to pay

my debts, which were three pounds; and he assured
me he would never expect the money again. But in
less than a month he came and demanded it; and
when I assured him I had nothing to pay he threatened to sell me. Though I knew he had no right to
do that, yet as I had no friend in the world to go to,
it alarmed me greatly.[159]

To get money, Gronniosaw went on something called
"privateering" – he served as a cook aboard an armed pri-
vately owned ship authorized by the government to attack
merchant ships of hostile nations. At the end of their campaign, after they returned to New York he was to receive
one hundred and thirty five pounds and some sugar. But
the man he owed three pounds went with him to the place
he would be paid and took all this for himself. The captain
of the ship was angry about this but did nothing, possibly,
because the young gentleman was a business associate of
his. Another man wanted to intervene, as Gronniosaw
describes here:

> At this time a very worthy gentleman, a wine mer-
> chant; his name was Dunscum, took me under his
> protection, and would have recovered my money for
> me if I had chose it; but I told him to let it alone;
> that I would rather be quiet. I believed that it would
> not prosper with him; and so it happened, for by
> a series of losses and misfortunes he became poor,
> and was soon after drowned on a party of pleasure.
> The vessel was driven out to sea, and struck against
> a rock, by which means every soul perished.[160]

Gronniosaw's point appears to be that even though he would not fight for himself, God, in his own mysterious ways would fight for him.

A second mysterious incident was, in fact, on the ship where Gronniosaw made the money that was cruelly taken from him. It had to do with one of the sailors.

> I met with many enemies, and much persecution, among the sailors; one of them was very unkind to me, and studied ways to vex and tease me. I cannot help mentioning one circumstance that hurt me more than all the rest, which was, that he snatched a book out of my hand that I was very fond of, and used frequently to amuse myself with, and threw it into the sea. But what is remarkable he was the first that was killed in our engagement. I do not pretend to say that this happened because he was not my friend: but I thought 't was a very awful providence to see how the enemies of the Lord are cut off.[161]

This was for Gronniosaw yet another example of how God would act mysteriously to punish wicked people. He had no doubt this sailor was a wicked man, because he had personal experience of it.

Gronniosaw's awareness of the mysterious ways God fights for him influenced his response to some of the situations he encountered. One occasion was when the woman he gave 25 guineas to keep for him denied she ever received the money. Another woman, who heard about this, intervened on Gronniosaw's behalf and "would have used some tougher means" to get it, but Gronniosaw did not want her to, "'Let it go', says I, 'My God is in heaven'".[162]

Hence, Gronniosaw's story shows that he saw God as his ever-present protector. God protected him by giving him kind masters and eliminating those who treated him badly. His portrayal of slave maters in very good light, which might sound curious to some readers, can be understood from the point of view that he saw them as Gods' agents for helping him. He also saw God as all-powerful. To him, there was nothing beyond God. This belief is the root of the strong inner resolve he often demonstrated when faced with adversity. Finally, Gronniosaw, perhaps more than any of the other three saw God as a spiritual being, who acts beyond the physical, visible realm. This can be seen in some of the links he made in his story, such as when the seaman who often treated him badly, was the first to be killed when the fighting began. Gronniosaw saw this as punishment by God.

Equiano the Activist

A key aspect of Equiano's understanding of God is the sense that God is everywhere, and can see our thoughts our actions. He believed that God was often working behind the scene either to support those things God likes or to thwart schemes that did not meet God' approval. Equiano gave this example of how the hand of God can work to safeguard people aboard a ship he was on:

> I belonged for a few days in the year 1758 to the *Jason*, of fifty-four guns, at Plymouth; and one night, when I was on board, a woman with a child

at her breast, fell from the upper-deck down into the hold, near the keel. Every one thought that the mother and child must be both dashed to pieces; but, to our great surprise, neither of them was hurt. I myself one day fell headlong from the upper-deck of the *Aetna* down the afterhold, when the ballast was out; and all who saw me fall cried out I was killed: but I received not the least injury. And in the same ship a man fell from the masthead on the deck without being hurt. In these, and in many more instances, I thought I could plainly trace the hand of God, without whose permission a sparrow cannot fall.[163]

He believed that God not only knew and saw everything, but was also bringing out his will at every nook and cranny of the world. If he became ill, it was because God allowed it to happen, and if he got better, it was because God wanted it to be so. He gives this description of an illness he had when he first came to London:

Though I had desired so much to see London, when I arrived in it I was unfortunately unable to gratify my curiosity; for I had at this time the chilblains to such a degree that I could not stand for several months, and I was obliged to be sent to St George's Hospital. There, I grew so ill, that the doctors wanted to cut my left leg off at different times, apprehending a mortification; but I always said I would rather die than suffer it; and happily (I thank God) I recovered without the operation.[164]

At another time when he became ill with fever, it was to God he appealed. He even made a promise to God of how he would live if he got better:

> I caught a fever and ague. I was very ill for eleven days and near dying; eternity was now exceedingly impressed on my mind, and I feared very much that awful event. I prayed the Lord therefore to spare me; and I made a promise in my mind to God, that I would be good if ever I should recover. At length, from having an eminent doctor to attend me, I was restored again to health; and soon after we got the vessel loaded, and set off for Montserrat.[165]

But with a poetic remark that reminds one of Sancho, he confesses finding this promise difficult to keep.

> During the package, as I was perfectly restored, and had much business of the vessel to mind, all my endeavours to keep up my integrity, and perform my promise to God, began to fail; and, in spite of all I could do, as we drew nearer and nearer to the island, my resolutions more and more declined, as if the very air of that country or climate seemed fatal to piety. When we were safe arrived at Montserrat, and I had got ashore, I forgot my former resolutions. – Alas! how prone is the heart to leave that God it wishes to love! and how strongly do the things of this world strike the senses and captivate the soul![166]

His sense that God is everywhere and in everything can also be seen in this incident aboard a ship, which he recalls:

> While I was in this ship an incident happened, which, though trifling, I beg leave to relate, as I could not help taking particular notice of it, and considering it then as a judgement of God. One morning a young man was looking up to the fore-top, and in a wicked tone, common on shipboard, d-d (sic) his eyes about something. Just at the moment some small particles of dirt fell into his left eye, and by the evening it was very much inflamed. The next day it grew worse; and within six or seven days he lost it.[167]

Even though what this young fellow did wrong is not clear to us, it was clearly something Equiano saw as wrong, and God not only saw it but punished it swiftly.

This takes us into another important aspect of Equiano's understanding of who God is, one which has been referred to in an earlier chapter – God's justice. Equiano believed that God was just and this shows itself in his writing in two ways. First, because God is just, God will not let evil go unpunished. For example, in the Caribbean, where he saw much cruelty, he was convinced their sins were "enough to bring down God's judgement"[168]. It was also a key aspect of his engagement publicly with the issue of slavery later in his life. When he attacked a supporter of the slave trade, Mr J Tobin, in a newspaper article, it was one of his points. He writes:

You will not I am sure, escape the upbraiding of your conscience, unless you are fortunate enough to have none; and remember also, that the oppressor and the oppressed are in the hands of the just and awful God, who says, Vengeance is mine and I will repay - repay the oppressor and the justifier of the oppression. How dreadful then will your fate be? The studied and torturing punishments, inhuman, as they are, of a barbarous planter, or a more barbarous overseer, will be tenderness compared to the provoked wrath of an angry but righteous God! who will raise, I have the fullest confidence, many of the sable race to the joys of Heaven, and cast the oppressive white to that doleful place, where he will cry, but will cry in vain, for a drop of water![169]

On the other hand, God blesses those who do the right thing, as can be seen in this reference to Granville Sharp, Rev James Ramsey and the Quakers, who were white people fighting for the slaves. This is contained in another newspaper article written by Equiano addressed to "the Senate of Great Britain"

To that truly immortal and illustrious advocate of our liberty, Granville Sharp, Esq., the philanthropist and justly Reverend James Ramsay, and the much to be honoured body of gentlemen called Friends, who have exerted every endeavour to break the accused yoke of Slavery, and ease the heavy burdens of the oppressed Negroes. "Those that honour their Maker have mercy on the Poor"; - and many blessing are upon the head of the just.[170]

On some occasions he pronounced this blessings himself. In the same newspaper article that he notes God's blessings for Sharp, Ramsay and the Quakers, he also writes:

> It is righteousness exalteth a nation, but sin is a reproach to any people. – Destruction shall be to the workers of iniquity – and the wicked shall perish by their own wickedness. – May the worthy Lord Bishop of London be blessed for his [sympathetic] and humane sermon on behalf of the Africans, and all the benevolent gentlemen who are engaged in the laudable attempt to abolish Slavery.[171]

Equiano's belief that God is just shows itself, secondly, in the way he uses the same measure for others as for himself. The tendency for God to punish sin was not just something for other people to experience; it happened to him too. In other words, God was fair. In his view, God did not practice favouritism.

> God looks with equal good-will on all his creatures, whether black or white – let neither, therefore, arrogantly condemn the other.[172]

The only thing that guaranteed a person God's favour was the way the person lived. This was why, as we saw above, he promised to live right when he was ill with fever. Sometimes when he met a misfortune, he would believe this was a judgement from God for something he had done wrong. For example, when he was sold, unexpectedly, by his master, which meant a return to the brutal slavery of the Caribbean islands, he was convinced this was because of something he had done wrong:

> I must have done something to displease the Lord, that he thus punished me so severely. This filled me with painful reflections on my past conduct... I felt that the Lord was able to disappoint me in all things, and immediately considered my present situation as a judgement of Heaven.[173]

Equiano's belief that God is just can also be seen in his wholehearted trust in the will of God for his life. He even left in God's hands his freedom, which by his own admission, was more precious than his life. He rejected offers and opportunities to escape from his masters, preferring to gain his freedom by honest means; since that is what would please God. After he was sold in London back into the harsh slavery of the Caribbean islands, he still resisted temptations to escape:

> The reader cannot but judge of the irksomeness of this situation to a mind like mine, in being daily exposed to new hardships and impositions, after having seen many better days, and having been as it were in a state of freedom and plenty; added to which, every part of the world I had hitherto been in seemed to me a paradise in comparison of the West Indies. My mind was therefore hourly replete with inventions and thoughts of being freed, and, if possible, by honest and honourable means; for I always remembered the old adage; and I trust it has ever been my ruling principle, that honesty is the

best policy; and likewise that other golden precept – to do unto all men as I would they should do unto me.[174]

He worked hard to get enough money to buy his freedom and prayed to God:

> In the midst of these thoughts I therefore looked up with prayers anxiously to God for my liberty; and at the same time I used every honest means, and endeavoured all that was possible on my part to obtain it. In process of time I became master of a few pounds, and in a fair way of making more, which my friendly captain knew very well; this occasioned him sometimes to take liberties with me: but whenever he treated me waspishly I used plainly to tell him my mind, and that I would die before I would be imposed on as other negroes were, and that to me life had lost its relish when liberty was gone.[175]

So it could be said that, Equiano's writings show that he had a strong sense of God's omnipresence. This can be seen in the care he took to record different events. He acknowledged as much in at the end of his book:

> My life and fortune have been extremely chequered, and my adventures various. Even those I have related are considerably abridged. If any incident in this little work should appear uninteresting and trifling to most readers, I can only say, as my excuse for mentioning it, that almost every event of my life made an impression on my mind and influenced my

conduct. I early accustomed myself to look for the hand of God in the most minor occurrence, and to learn from it a lesson of morality and religion; and in this light every circumstance I have related was to me of importance.[176]

In constantly having his mind on God, Equiano was like Gronniosaw. But he differed with Gronniosaw in the way he thought about God's justness. Gronniosaw was more likely to think that God was on his side and that he, as an individual, was in God's favour. Equiano, on the other hand, appeared to believe he did not deserve God's favour any more than anybody else. For him God was not only righteous, that is, rewarding good and punishing evil, God was also fair, that is, applying the same standard to all people. For him, it is only living right with God and doing good deeds that can guarantee anybody the protection of God.

Equiano's life was possibly shaped by this understanding of God. He was extremely hard working. As a slave, his work was directed at making money for his master. But he worked hard enough to make sufficient money on the side to buy his freedom twice over. He also often made so much money for those who were his masters, that they were usually reluctant to lose him. Even after he bought his freedom and came to live in London, he spent the rest of his life as a tireless campaigner against slavery; writing and selling his books in speaking tours which took him all over Great Britain and Ireland. He visited parliament with other black leaders to lobby MPs, spoke at abolitionists meetings, debated supporters of slavery on the newspapers and so on. The same attitude towards his own slavery seems to characterise his approach to abolition, namely, to look to God for deliverance, but work hard in the meantime to achieve it.

Cugoano the Visionary

The best way to describe Cugoano's understanding of God is that he saw God as the "Almighty Creator". Of the four Africans being studied, Cugoano had the strongest sense of the cosmic dimension of God, the sense that God was Lord of the universe whose power reaches everywhere. He often used the world "Almighty" to refer to God, as in "Almighty Creator" or "Almighty Redeemer", and speaks of God as "Omnipotent", "High" and "Sovereign." For example, he writes, "This must be observed, that it hath so pleased the Almighty Creator, to establish all the variety of things in nature, different complexions and other circumstances among men…"[177]

In considering how Africans might be saved from slavery, he urged the British to help, but if not:

> …it is our duty to look up to a greater deliverer than that of the British nation, or of any nation upon earth; for unless God gives them repentance, and peace towards him, we can expect no peace or deliverance from them. But still we shall have cause to trust, that God who made of one blood all the nations and children of men, and who gave to all equally providential justice, shall then make enlargement and deliverance to arise to the grievously injured, and heavy oppressed Africans from another place.[178]

His consciousness of the cosmic dimensions of God
has the result that his concepts tend to be on a cosmic
scale. For example, after suggesting that a way of taking Christianity to non-Christian nations is by having
the Bible translated into the language of those countries
and setting up a college to give theological training to
the people who would be sent there, he remarked that
"many Anti-Christian errors" and "false philosophy which
abounds among Christians" are the possible hindrance to
this. These errors seem to:

> ...threaten with an universal deluge; but God hath
> promised to fill the world with a knowledge of him-
> self, and he hath set up his bow in the rational heav-
> ens, as well as in the clouds, as a token that he will
> stop the proud ways of error and delusion.[179]

In other words, God will act from heaven to cancel
the effect on the world of both non-Christian ideas and
erroneous Christian thinking that might oppose the idea
of spreading Christianity by translating the Bible into
other languages.

Evidence of the sense of God as a cosmic being, can
also be seen in the way Cugoano refers to heaven in his
writing. For example, he talks about the injustice done to
slaves crying out to heaven:

> For the wickedness that you [the British] have done
> is great, and wherever you traffic and colonies have
> been extended it is shameful; and the great injus-
> tice and cruelty done to the poor Africans crieth
> to heaven against you; and therefore that it may be

forgiven unto you, it cries aloud for universal refor-
mation and national repentance.[180]

He quotes an unnamed writer who begs God to hear
these cries:

> Gracious God! How wicked, how beyond all exam-
> ple impious, must be that servitude which cannot
> be carried on without the continual murder of so
> many innocent persons. What punishment is not to
> be expected from such monstrous and unparralled
> barbarity? For if the blood of one man unjustly shed
> cries with so loud a voice for the Divine vengeance,
> how shall the cries and groans of an hundred thou-
> sand men annually murdered ascend the celestial
> mansions, and bring down punishment such enor-
> mities deserve?[181]

Law was also a key part of how Cugoano saw God.
He believed that the God that made the world has ordered
everything to work according to his law. These laws of
God operating within all that God has made, should
therefore be the basis for national laws. One of his strongest lines of criticism against slavery was that it went
against the laws of God. He writes:

> No necessity, or any situation of men, however poor,
> pitiful and wretched they may be, can warrant them
> to rob others, or oblige them to become thieves,
> because they are poor, miserable and wretched: But
> the robbers of men, the kidnappers, enslavers and
> slave-holders, who take away the common rights
> and privileges of others to support and enrich them-

selves, are universally those pitiful and detestable wretches; for the ensnaring of others, taking away their liberty by slavery and oppression, is the worst kind of robbery, as most opposite to every precept and injunction of the Divine Law.

He explains the specific laws of God which are disobeyed, by pointing out that such behaviour is:

> Contrary to that command which enjoins that *all men should love their neighbours as themselves,* and *that they should do unto others, as they would that men should do to them.* [182]

He uses two hypothetical scenarios to bring home the point of the Golden Rule:

> Suppose that some of the African pirates had been as dextrous as the European, and that they had made excisions on the coast of Great Britain or elsewhere…and that they should carry off your sons and your daughters, and your wives and friends, to a perpetual and barbarous slavery, you would certainly think that those African pirates were justly deserving of any punishment that could be put upon them. But the European pirates and merchandizers …have no better right to steal, kidnap, buy, and carry away and sell the Africans, than the Africans would have to carry away any of the Europeans in the same barbarous and unlawful manner.[183]

Elsewhere, he makes other references to God's laws:

Thus saith the law of God: if a man be found stealing any of his neighbours, or he that stealeth a man (let him be who he will) and selleth him, or that taketh merchandize of him, or if he be found in his hand, then that thief shall die. However, in modern slavery among Christians, who ought to know this law, they have not had any regard for it. Surely if any law among them admits of death as a punishment for robbing or defrauding others of their money or goods, it ought to be double death, if was possible, when a man is robbed of himself, and sold into captivity and cruel slavery.[184]

Cugoano's conviction that slave traders were disobeying a good and powerful God made him issue many dire warnings for what could happen to them if they continued with this:

,,,this must appear evident, that for any man to carry on a traffic in the merchandize of slaves, and to keep them in slavery; or for any nation to oppress, extirpate and destroy others; that these are crimes of the greatest magnitude, and a most daring violation of the laws and commandments of the Most High, and which, at last, will be evidenced in the destruction and overthrow of all the transgressors. And nothing else can be expected for such violations of taking away the natural rights and liberties of men, but that those who are the doers of it will meet with some awful visitation of the righteous judgement of God...[185]

Yet another important aspect of his understanding of God is the issue of diversity in creation. Cugoano believed that God was a creator who loved diversity. This link between creation and diversity is, in fact, part of everyday language today. We would describe as "creative" an artwork that contained many different shapes and sizes, or many different colours. This was how Cugoano saw God. Time and time he reminds his readers that God deliberately made people to have different complexions, "This must be observed, that it hath so pleased the Almighty Creator, to establish all the variety of things in nature, different complexions and other circumstances among men…"[186]

This belief that God was pleased with diversity, was why he supported that Africans should retain their African names within Christianity. Even though God wanted humans to live according to laws, God did not have a restricted outlook to the world, wanting everything to be chosen from a small list and contained within a small space. Rather, God is a being that wanted humans to thrive and be who they are.

This can be seen in his determination to maintain his Africanness against the pressures of British life. Of the four Africans being studied, Cugoano appears to have been the most reluctant to give up his African names. His story suggests that he only gave up the names Ottobah Cugoano, to adopt the European names, John Stuart, because there was the danger that he might be taken back into slavery if he retained those African names. In some of the letters to white or black abolitionist colleagues that he signed or co-signed, he used both names, Ottobah

Cugoano and John Stuart. When he wrote his book *Thoughts and Sentiments*, he wrote his name as Ottobah Cugoano. For this committed Christian, this was a clear indication that he did not think he needed to be anything other than African to be acceptable to God.

Cugoano's knowledge of God's love for diversity made him take the view that whenever Christianity was being taken from Europe to another culture, only the core substance of the faith should be carried over. The recipients should be allowed to develop their own ceremonies:

> Teaching would be exceedingly necessary to the pagan nations and ignorant people in every place and situation, but they do not need any unscriptural forms and ceremonies to be taught unto them; they can devise superstitions enough among themselves, and church government too, if ever they need any.[187]

In other words, any people and place receiving the Christian religion have the right to dispense with the cultural and traditional baggage it came with and to take on their own culture. Interestingly, many people today still treat this as a radical idea, but Cugoano was saying it over 200 years ago. Yet another indication of how much of a visionary he was.

Cugoano's conviction that God delighted in seeing a creation full of many different things, in different shapes, sizes and colours; and in particular, people of different sizes, shapes and complexions was probably why he was so sure God will punish those who enslave Africans because

they were black. They were in effect opposing God, who
had deliberately made people different.

> We may be assured that God will certainly avenge
> himself of such heinous transgressors of his law,
> and of all those planters and merchants, and of all
> others, who are the authors of the Africans graves,
> severities, and cruel punishments, and no plea of
> any absolute necessity can possibly excuse them.[188]

Cugoano knew some of these would come across as
harsh, but he believed there was no easy way of saying it.
For example, after comparing slave traders with robbers
he writes:

> This may seem a harsh comparison, but the parallel
> is so coincident that, I must say, I can find no other
> way of expressing my Thoughts and Sentiments,
> without making use of some harsh words and com-
> parisons against the carriers on of such abandoned
> wickedness. But, in this little undertaking, I must
> humbly hope the impartial reader will excuse such
> defects as may arise from want of better education;
> and as to the resentment.[189]

But Cugoano's words never came out of a feeling of
vindictiveness. Rather, it was his apprehension of the danger looming ahead of the British due to the wickedness
of slavery. His words were meant as a warning to those
involved to mend their ways:

> It is therefore necessary that the inhabitants of the
> British nation should seriously consider these things

for their own good and safety, as well as for our benefit and deliverance, and that they may be sensible of their own error and danger, lest they provoke the vengeance of the Almighty against them.[190]

From the above, we can say that Ottobah Cugoano had an immense sense of God's power and reach across the universe. This was why he used words like "Almighty", "Most High" and "Sovereign" to refer to God. It was also why he tended to see farther ahead than those around him, and think at a much larger scale about things. It was this sense of the immense power of God that was at the root of his radicalism. He also saw God as good and as one who abhors evil. This gave him the immense sense that those who were engaged in slave trading were walking a dangerous path; God will not allow that disobedience forever. Another important aspect of his understanding of God is as lover of a variety or diversity. He points out that God deliberately made people to have different complexions because God was pleased by these differences. To enslave people, therefore, because they have different characteristics is to be in direct opposition to God.

Concluding Remarks

As we did in the previous chapter, we will conclude by imagining a joint presentation by these four Africans on how they understand God. Sancho, if he goes first, would probably start by saying that God is a Generous Giver of good things. He would give the example of how God gave him the opportunity to learn to read and write by taking him away from a wicked family to a kind one, how God has given good health and good character to people he knows. He would recall how "every good affection, every sweet sensibility, every heart-felt joy – humanity, politeness, charity" come from God. He would also point out that God not only provides but protects and for that reason is to be trusted.

The theme of protection would be picked up by Gronniosaw if he went second. He would describe God as the Great Protector and tell of the many instances when God had protected him, such as when God "melted" the heart of an African king to spare Gronniosaw from being beheaded and when God made a Colchester lawyer to come looking for him and his family thus saving them from starvation. He would probably exclaim, perhaps with a shake of the head, "O the boundless mercies of my GOD!" He would also describe how God had protected him by giving him good masters, beginning with the Dutch captain who, by buying him saved him from being killed, to Mr Freelandhouse, who gave him his freedom. He would also point to the power of God by which God does many miracles and how this has been the root of his strong trust in God. Finally, he would say how God is a Spirit, not a physical being, and describe how he, himself, has had mysterious experiences of God.

Equiano would move the presentation from the personal to the social. He would agree that God is personal, and might even give examples of how God has saved him from many perilous voyages. He would, however, point out that partly because of all the evils of slavery he has witnessed, what mattered to him the most is that God is just. God was fair to all, black or white, old or young, man or woman. What, ultimately, attracts God's favour to anyone is whether they are living right with God. He would also point out his belief that God is everywhere, seeing everything and bringing out his will in the world through different events. This was the basis of his trust in God. He has been able to not only trust God with his life, but with something more important – his freedom.

Cugoano would continue along this line, extending it further. He would point out the cosmic dimension of God's activities and concerns. He would describe God with words like "Creator", "Almighty", "Sovereign", "High" and "Omnipotent" to capture this sense of a being in overall control of everything. He would describe how God has ordered the universe according to law and how God can act from heaven to put things right in the world Cugoano would also point out that God was a lover of diversity and how this is a major point against the slave trade. Those trading in Africans as slaves because they have a dark complexion are in direct contradiction to God who made them dark because he wanted human beings to have different complexions. He would finish by saying that it was for this reason that he has supported African Christians retaining their African names. He did not see any contradiction in retaining the African heritage and being a Christian since it was God that made Africa.

CHAPTER 5:

UNDERSTANDING OF HUMANITY

One idea that affects people's behaviour much more than they realise is their understanding of humanity, that is, what they think a human being is. I recently heard a story of a village that discovered a newborn baby abandoned in a remote corner of the village. The baby was dead when it was discovered. Nobody knew where she had come from or what her name was. The villagers collectively gave the baby a name and paid for a proper funeral at which most of them turned up. The person telling the story made the point that in their actions towards the baby, the villages were showing what they understood a human being to be. This illustrates the point that the understanding of what a human being is influences the way people behave to each other. In this chapter we will try to discern how our four Africans understood what a human is by studying how they behaved towards people. In addition to their behaviour toward people, we will also draw from what they have written explicitly on the issue.

Sancho the Poet

Sancho's attitude, which is visible behind his actual words, shows that for him, a human being should be a force for good in the world; something that increases goodness around it. It is this "humanity" that flows out of Sancho's letters; and this was probably why people kept asking him for more of it. The American who wanted to publish Sancho's letters made that very point in his letter to Sancho:

> The principal view I have in addressing these by letter, is to inform thee that there have lately fallen in my hands two letters of thy writing, the one to a gentleman in the East Indies, the other to my friend Jabez Fisher from Philadelphia.
>
> I am so pleased with these letters, on account of the humanity and strong good sense they contain, that I am very desirous of gaining thy permission to print them in a collection of Letters of Friendship, which I think of publishing in autumn. I have thy two letters in my possession, but did not think it would be acting candidly to publish them without thy consent, which I am very solicitous to obtain.[191]

There are many examples of this outpouring of "humanity" in Sancho's letters. In a letter to one Mrs. H (full name not known), Sancho writes:

Dear Madam

Your son, who is a welcome visitor wherever he comes, made himself more welcome to me by the kind proof of your regard he brought in his hands. – Souls like yours, who delight in giving pleasure, enjoy a heaven on earth; for I am convinced, that the disposition of the mind in a great measure forms either the heaven or hell in both worlds.[192]

It is also possible to see the effect of his letters in the writings of other people. This is what one George Cumberland wrote in a letter after meeting with Sancho:

I must tell you (because it pleases my vanity so to do) that a Black Man, Ignatius Sancho, has lately put me into an unbounded conceit with myself – he is said to be a great judge of literary performances (God send it may be true!) and has praised my Tale of Cambambo and Journal wh (sic) I read to him, so highly, that I shall like him as long as I live – nothing less than publishing I fear will satisfy him – but what would not one do to satisfy so good a kind of man? – In the mean time as he is a grocer I think it would be proper to buy all my Tea and Sugar of him...[193]

His friends, from all indication, could not get enough of this outpouring of goodwill – this "humanity". At least one of Sancho's letters to young Jack Wingrave was from a request from Jack's father. Hence, Sancho writes, "You good father insists on my scribbling a sheet of absurdities, and gives me a notable reason for it, that is, 'Jack will be pleased with it.'"[194]

Sancho's writings show him not only overflowing with good wishes to other, but from time to time, with gratitude. Here is a letter he wrote to one Mr John Spink regarding a gift:

> In truth, I was never more puzzled in my life than at this very present writing – The acts of common kindness, or the effusions of mere common good-will, I should know what to reply to – but, by my conscience, you act upon so grand a scale of urbanity, that a man should possess a mind as noble and a heart as ample as yourself, before he attempts even to be grateful upon paper.[195]

His writings also show him to be very self-aware about his tendency to praise and bless people. He praised people because he believed the world needed such expression of goodwill. In another letter to young Mr Wingrave, in 1786, Sancho writes, regarding praise, "Mankind are not too lavish of it – censure is dealt out by wholesale, while praise is very sparingly distributed – Nine times in ten mankind may err in their blame – but in its praises the world is seldom, if ever, mistaken."[196]

The indication is that he was also a man that is able to forgive those who have offended him and ask for forgiveness from those he has offended. In a letter to one Mr G (full name not known) he writes:

> Sir
>
> The very handsome manner in which you have apologized for your late lapse of behaviour does you credit. – Contrition, the child of conviction, serves

to prove the goodness of your heart – The man of levity often errs – but it is the man of sense alone who can gracefully acknowledge it. – I accept your apology - and if in the manly heat of wordy contest aught escaped my lips tinged with undue asperity, I ask your pardon, and hope you will mutually exchange forgiveness with.[197]

On the surface, Sancho's attitude can appear nonchalant. When read deeply, however, his letters show that Sancho's generosity springs from a very low opinion of earthly life, often found among Christians. In a letter to his good friend, Mr Meheux, on August 7, 1768 he writes:

Lord! What is man? – and what business have such lazy, lousy, paltry beings of a day to dorm friendships, or to make connexions? Man is an absurd animal – yea, I will ever maintain it – in his vices, dreadful – in his few virtues, silly – religious without devotion – philosophy without wisdom – the divine passion (as it is called) love too oft without affection – and anger without cause – friendship without reason – hate without reflection – knowledge…without judgment – and wit without discretion.[198]

Sancho's point is that on their own human beings are fickle and without substance. They have dreadful vices, few virtues, empty, religious attitude that do not arise from genuine devotion to God, they try to put forward philosophical ideas, but it is not based on real wisdom, their love they appear to show has no real affection behind it and so on.

In another letter, he makes reference to Psalm 144:3, to make the point that it is God who makes human life worthwhile. King David: the writer of the Psalm realised this and gave gratitude to God, but other human beings did not always:

> Smoking my morning pipe, the friendly warmth of glorious planet the sun – the leniency of the air – the cheerful glow of the atmosphere – made me involuntarily cry, "Lord, what is man that thou in thy mercy art so mindful of him! Or what the son of man, that thou in thy mercy art so mindful of him! David whose heart and affections were naturally of the first kind…pours forth the grateful sentiments of his enraptured soul in the sweetest, modulations of [sympathetic] oratory. The tender mercies of the Almighty are not less to many of his creatures – but their hearts, unlike the royal disposition of the shepherd king, are cold, and untouched with the sweet ray of gratitude.[199]

Sancho, very much longed for heaven, a much better world than this:

> Poor Lady S, I find still lingers this side [of] the world. – Alas! when will the happy period arrive that the sons of morality may greet each other with the joyful news, that sin, pain, sorrow, and death, are no more! skies without clouds, earth without crimes, life without death, world without end! –

peace, bliss, and harmony, where the Lord – God –
All in all – King of kings – Lord of lords – reigneth
– omnipotent – for ever – for ever! – May you, dear
Meheux, and all I love –yea the whole race of Adam,
join with my unworthy, weak self, in the stupen-
dous – astonishing – soul-cheering Hallelujahs! [200]

His belief that there was a better world contributed to
his low view of this world and the value of life within it.

Another aspect of Sancho's thinking on humanity is
that all human beings are part of one family. This can be
seen in the longing for the joining together of "the whole
race of Adam" with himself and his friend Meheux in
soul-cheering Hallelujahs in heaven. In another letter to
one Mr Fisher in America, thanking him for books highlighting the plight of African slaves,[201] Sancho writes:

I, who, thank God! am no bigot – but honour virtue – and the practice of the great moral duties
– equally in the turban – or the lawn-slaves[202] –
who think Heaven big enough for all the race of
man – and hope to see and mix amongst the whole
family of Adam in bliss hereafter – I with these
notions (which, perhaps, some may style absurd)
look upon the friendly Author [of the books] – as
a being far superior to any great name upon your
continent.[203]

In the context of slavery, he thinks of humanity as
being of the same family; and all people as welcome to
heaven. It can also be inferred from his "thank God am
not a bigot" and his remark that he values people whether

in turban or lawn-sleeves, that is, notwithstanding where they come from, that he considers prejudice deplorable.

This attitude to prejudice can be seen in a letter Sancho wrote to a young family friend, Jack Wingrave. The young man, who was in India at the time, had apparently written home complaining about the behaviour of the natives. He described the natives as a set of "deceitful people" who did not know "such a word as Gratitude".[204] Sancho, in his own letter, pointed out to him that most of the bad habits of the natives were passed on to them by European visitors to their land. Then he added:

> I mentioned these only to guard my friend against being too hasty in condemning the knavery of a people, who, bad as they may be – possibly – were made worse by their Christian visitors. – Make human nature [thy] study, wherever thou residest – whatever the religion, or the complexion, study their hearts. – Simplicity, kindness, and charity be thy guide! – With these even Savages will respect you – and God will bless you.[205]

In conclusion, Sancho demonstrated his understanding by his attitude towards other people, which can also be perceived behind his words. His attitude shows that for Sancho, a human being is a positive creative force in nature. Behind his written words is a man whose heart was bursting with goodwill and gratitude towards people. He also demonstrated this understanding in his love of the arts, a love he expressed in his poetic writings. Close analysis shows that this generosity was rooted in a Christian understanding of human beings and of life on earth as not worth much for their own sake. For example, he saw the human being as nothing without God, which is an echo of the Psalms. This was greatly influenced by his view of heaven which was often at the back of his mind. This image meant that when discussing slavery, he saw human beings as being like one family, all descendants of Adam.

Gronniosaw the Noble

In the same way, Sancho's letters give valuable insight into his ideas, we can learn about Gronniosaw's understanding of humanity by studying what he said about himself. We should not expect grand statements about the nature of human beings because his book was not a book of philosophy. What we have, rather, is a man's story about the travails of life and how God acted time and time to protect him. Because he concentrates so much on God, what comes across in his book is that he understands human beings essentially as creatures living under the mercy of God. When he tells the story of wicked people, the story often ends with their untimely and horrible death. The man who tormented him when he worked as a cook on a battle ship, who in one instance snatched a book Gronniosaw loved very much and threw it into the sea, met a terrible death. Also, the young gentleman that gave him money, telling him he did not need to pay it back, but then came back and not only took from Gronniosaw what he had lent him but, in fact, took all the money Gronniosaw made aboard a ship, which was many times more than the fellow had given to Gronniosaw, died a short time later in an accident. Although Gronniosaw did not say this, explicitly, the feeling one gets from his story was that it was the bad things these two men did that had caught up with them.

This view partly explains the way he treated those people who offended him. One example was when Gronniosaw came to England and gave money to a publican to keep for him and she later denied she ever received it. This is Gronniosaw's account of what happened:

> I inquired if any serious Christian people resided there, the woman I made this inquiry of, answered me in the affirmative; and added, that she was one of them. I was heartily glad to hear her say so. I thought I could give her my whole heart; she kept a public house. I deposited with her all the money that I had not an immediate occasion for; as I thought it would be safer with her. It was 25 guineas, but 6 of them I desired her to lay out to the best advantage, to buy me some shirts, a hat and some other necessaries. I made her a present of a large handsome large looking-glass that I brought with me from Martinico, in order to recompense her for the trouble I had given her. I must do this woman the justice to acknowledge that she did lay out some little for my use, but the 19 guineas and part of the 6 guineas with my watch, she would not return, but denied that I ever gave it her.[206]

Gronniosaw was, clearly, not in a strong position as a black man living at time when slavery was still legal. It is, however, noticeable that even when people wanted to intervene on his behalf, he often objected. For example, when somebody offered to recover his money from the young gentleman who had taken all the money he made from privateering in America, he declined the offer. Similarly, he did not totally pursue the offer to recover his money from this publican lady when the offer was made:

> This publican had a brother who lived on Portsmouth Common, his wife was a very serious good woman. When she heard of the treatment I had met with, she came and inquired into my real situation, and was greatly troubled at the ill usage I had received, and took me home to her own house. I began now to rejoice, and my prayer was turned into praise. She made use of all the arguments in her power to prevail on her who had wronged me to return my watch and money, but it was to no purpose, as she had given me no receipt, and I had nothing to show for it, I could not demand it. My good friend was excessively angry with her, and obliged her to give me back four guineas, which she said she gave me out of charity; though in fact it was my own and much more: She would have employed some rougher means to obliged her to give up my money, but I would not suffer her: let it go, says I, "My God is in heaven."[207]

Gronniosaw probably sees all human existence as sustained by the generosity of God. In a manner of speaking, everybody is living at God's expense. Those who act badly, like the two men whose life were extinguished, eventually run out of credit.

This means that Gronniosaw's understanding of humanity is not separable from his understanding of God. Because he saw human beings, primarily, as creatures living under the mercy of God, he craved God's protection.

Another important part of Gronniosaw's understanding of the human being, which has already been hinted at above, is that human beings are nothing without God. This is quite similar to what was seen in Sancho's understanding. But it is much stronger in Gronniosaw's understanding. He was particularly conscious of his own sinfulness and worthlessness before God. This was evident during the major religious crisis of his life, provoked by a sermon by his master, when he was still a slave.

> One Sunday; I heard my master preach from these words out of the Revelations, Chap i.7. "Behold, He cometh in the clouds and every eye shall see him, and they that pierced Him." These words affected me excessively: I was in great agony because I thought my master directed them to me only; and, I fancied, that he observed me with unusual earnestness. I was further confirmed in this belief, as I looked round the church, and could see no one person beside myself in such grief and distress as I was...[208]

He continued in this distressed state for some days until his mistress found out and gave him a book to read:

She gave me John Bonyan on the holy war, to read; I found his experience similar to my own, which gave me reason to suppose he must be a bad man; as I was convinced of my own corrupt nature, and the misery of my own heart...I took the book to my lady, and informed her I did not like it at all, as it was concerning a wicked man as bad as myself, I did not choose to read it, and I desired her to give me another, wrote by a better man, that was holy and without sin.[209]

He was given another book but this did not help either:

A few days after, my master gave me Baxter's Call to the Unconverted: This was no relief to me neither, on the contrary, it occasioned as much distress as the other had done before, *as it* invited all to come to *Christ* : and I found myself so wicked and miserable, that I could not come. This consideration threw me into agonies that cannot be described; insomuch, that I even attempted to put an end to my life. I took one of the large caseknives, and went into the stable, with an intent to destroy myself; and as I endeavoured with all my strength to force the knife into my side, it bent double. I was instantly struck with horror at the thoughts of my own rashness, and my conscience told me, that had I succeeded in this attempt, I should probably have gone to hell.[210]

This state of mind even made him physically ill for some days:

> I could find no relief, nor the least shadow of com-
> fort; the extreme distress of my mind so affected
> my health, that I continued ill for three days and
> nights, and would admit of no means to be taken
> for my recovery, though my lady was very kind, and
> sent many things to me: but I rejected every means
> of relief, and wished to die. I would not go into my
> own bed, but lay in the stable upon straw. I felt all
> the horrors of a troubled conscience, so hard to be
> borne, and saw all the vengeance of God ready to
> overtake me. I was sensible that there was no way for
> me to be saved unless I came to *Christ*, and I could
> not come to Him: I thought it was impossible he
> should receive such a sinner as me.[211]

He was in this state until he experienced Jesus Christ:

> The last night that I continued in this place, in
> the midst of my distress, these words were brought
> home upon my mind. Behold the Lamb of God.
> I was something comforted at this, and began to
> grow easier, and wished for day, that I might find
> these words in my Bible. I rose very early the fol-
> lowing morning, and went to my schoolmaster, Mr.
> Vanosdore, and communicated the situation of my
> mind to him; he was greatly rejoiced to find me
> inquiring the way to Zion, and blessed the Lord

who had worked so wonderfully for me, a poor heathen.[212]

At another time, Gronniosaw describe how he was distressed with:

> ...doubts, fears, and such a deep sense of my unworthiness, that after all the comfort and encouragement I had received, I was often tempted to believe I should be cast away at last. The more I saw of the beauty and glory of God, the more I was humbled under a sense of my own vileness.[213]

Although Gronniosaw was speaking about himself, his words give some indication of how he thinks human beings stand before God. He was a man who saw God in very glorious terms, and from all indication he saw human beings as being the exact opposite – small, sinful and insignificant without God.

These two aspects of Gronniosaw's thinking about the nature of human beings, that is, (a) human beings live under the mercy of God, and (b) human beings are worthless creatures on their own, fit together. Gronniosaw's own words capture this connection. When he was in deep distress about his sinfulness, he said, "I am very sensible that nothing but the great power and unspeakable mercies of the Lord could relieve my soul from the heavy burden it laboured under at that time."[214] His sense of worthlessness might appear over-the-top at times, but it is worth considering that such "over-the-top" worthlessness was the foundation of the strong faith that he was to have later on in life. Indeed, the very reason his story was published was to testify to that faith. It was felt by the publishers that his story "contains matter well worthy the notice and attention of every Christian reader."[215]

Gronniosaw's split between God and human beings, that is, God is good and big – humans are bad and small, commendable as it is, presented him with a problem when dealing with Christians. On the one hand, he saw Christians as the people of God, who God would use to protect him. For example, when he was discharged from the navy he was so determined to come to Britain, a Christian nation, and very much looked forward to living among Christians that he did not wait to collect his prize money:[216]

> I was then worth about thirty pounds, but I never regarded money in the least, nor would I tarry for my prize-money lest I should lose my chance of going to England. I went with the Spanish prisoners to Spain: and came to Old England with the English prisoners. I cannot describe my joy when we were within sight of Portsmouth… I expected to find nothing but goodness, gentleness and meekness in this Christian land.[217]

A similar inclination can be seen in his question to the publican from which his money trouble began, "I inquired if any serious Christian people resided there, the woman I made this inquiry of, answered me in the affirmative."[218] Another example is his description of becoming part of the Gilford household, after he returned to England from Switzerland. Even when he was joining the church, apart from looking forward to the opportunity to contemplate on the presence of God, there was a clear sense of him desiring to join the fellowship of Christians, "Soon after I came home, I waited on Doctor Gilford, who took me into his family, and was exceedingly good to me...I expressed a desire to be admitted into their church, and sit down with them.[219]

But Christians, being human beings, often disappointed him. This often resulted in an emotional/spiritual crisis, as he struggled to mentally adjust to that reality. For example, when the publican denied that Gronniosaw had given her money, his sadness was less about the money he lost, but more about being disappointed by a Christian, "Still I did not mind my loss in the least; all that grieved me was, that I had been disappointed in finding some Christian friends, with whom I hoped to enjoy a little sweet comfortable society."[220]

Something similar happened regarding Britain, for which he had very high hopes as a Christian country. First he was surprised to hear so many people swearing when he arrived at Portsmouth, then the publican took his money; when he was visiting London a "creditable" man took money from him just to show him his way. Reflecting, particularly on the publican's conduct, he writes:

> I could scarcely believe it possible that the place where so many eminent Christians had lived and preached could abound with so much wickedness and deceit. I thought it worse than *Sodom* (considering the great advantage they have) I cried like a child, and that almost continually: at length God heard my prayers, and raised me a friend indeed.[221]

From the above, it could be said that Gronniosaw understood what human beings are, mainly, with reference to God. His story shows that he saw human beings as living at God's mercy and under God's protection. He also saw human beings as being worthless, sinful creatures on their own. His sharp contrast between God and human beings often presented him with difficulties when dealing with Christians, who, on the one hand are God's people, but, on the other hand, are still human beings.

Equiano the Activist

Just as with the first two, Equiano's writing gives useful clues about what his understanding of humanity is, or what for him constitutes humanness. Sometimes this is plainly written in the book. Most times, it is simply operating behind the story. From the very first page, Equiano gives the course of humanity as one of the reasons for telling his story:

> I believe there are few events in my life, which have not happened to many: it is true the incidents of it are numerous; and, did I consider myself an European, I might say my sufferings were great: but when I compare my lot with that of most of my countrymen, I regard myself as a particular favourite of Heaven...I am not so foolishly vain as to expect from it either immortality or literary reputation. If it affords any satisfaction to my numerous friends, at whose request it has been written, or in the smallest degree promotes the interests of

humanity, the ends for which it was undertaken will
be fully attained.[222]

This, seemingly, innocuous introduction on the very
first page of the *Interesting Narrative* makes two important points. The first is that black and white people (or,
as Equiano put it, Europeans and "my countrymen") are
part of the same "humanity", the course of which the
book is hoped to promote. Yet, and this is the second
point, so different were their experiences that the level of
suffering which white people would consider great, would,
in the experience of black people seem so light that the
person concerned should regard himself a "favourite of
heaven."

After this, Equiano spent the rest of the chapter
describing the African people he came from. He gave its
location in Africa and described how the place was gov-
erned by chiefs and elders, who were physically marked
on the face:

> My father was one of those elders or chiefs I have
> spoken of, and was styled Embrenche; a term, as I
> remember, importing the highest distinction, and
> signifying in our language a *mark* of grandeur…I
> had seen it conferred on one of my brothers, and I
> was also *destined* to receive it by my parents.[223]

He went on to describe how the elders served as judges
and to give examples of some of the cases they decided on;
the marriage customs; the musical instruments the people
use and the way they dance; the "simple" manners and
"few" luxuries the people had, especially regarding cloth-

ing; the kind of food they ate and the way it is prepared; the type of buildings they lived in and how it was built; their "uncommonly rich and fruitful" land and the kind of crops produced on it; the way trade was conducted; the kind of weapons they had for fighting rival villages and how wars were fought; the religion of the people and how that impacted on the rest of their life and so on.

What he gives is a comprehensive description which locates the place geographically (he gives more information than I have included above) and describes its cultural, political and economic set up. Some instances he locates in his own family. For example, on the subject of religion, he described following his mother to make oblations at her mother's tomb:

> I was very fond of my mother, and almost constantly with her. When she went to make these oblations at her mother's tomb, which was a kind of small solitary thatched house, I sometimes attended her. There she made her libations, and spent most of the night in cries and lamentations.[224]

What Equiano was doing with this description is to tell the readers that he is a human being like them. Many British people would have, probably, seen a slave as coming from some distant land, somewhere in the "dark continent" of Africa. Equiano, says, "No, I have not come from some vague, notional place. I will tell you the particular place I come from. I will even locate it for you on the map of the world. What's more, we have a system of government like you do, a system of economics like you do, a way of life, which encompasses eating, clothing, dancing, marrying, delivering justice, fighting like you do, and a way of doing religion, like you do". In other words, he is saying to the reader, "I, a black African, I am a human being just like you."

Many of the episodes in Equiano's story relate to the issue of human dignity. In a section on the slavery in the West Indies, Equiano narrates many of the degradations he had seen:

> It was very common in several of the islands, particularly in St Kitt's, for the slaves to be branded with the initial letters of their master's name; and a load of heavy iron hooks hung about their necks. Indeed on the most trifling occasions they were loaded with chains; and often instruments of torture were added. The iron muzzle, thumb-screws, etc., are so well known, as not to need a description, and were sometimes applied for the slightest faults. I have seen a negro beaten till some of his bones were broken, for even letting a pot boil over.[225]

Equiano even recalled slaves being weighed like goods during a sale:

> I have often seen slaves, particularly those who were meagre, in different islands, put into scales and weighed; and then sold from three pence to six pence or nine pence a pound. My master, however, whose humanity was shocked at this mode, used to sell such by the lump. And at or after a sale it was not uncommon to see negroes taken from their wives, wives taken from their husbands,

and children from their parents, and sent off to other islands, and wherever else their merciless lords chose; and probably never more during life to see each other! Oftentimes my heart has bled at these partings; when the friends of the departed have been at the water side, and, with sighs and tears, have kept their eyes fixed on the vessel till it went out of sight.[226]

Equiano's statement at the beginning of the last extract, that the weighing of slaves shocked his master's "humanity" is an indication of his own belief that human beings should be treated with dignity. The weighing of a fellow human being, offended his master's sense of human dignity. Equiano would, also, have known that in the same way his master's sense of humanity was challenged by this incident, episode after episode of his life story would challenge the sense of dignity of his white British readers. So not only did he have clear understanding of humanity but he also knew how to use that understanding to good effect.

The acts of degradation he described were not restricted to slaves, but included those black people who have already bought their freedom. Equiano experienced some of it after he had bought his freedom. He gave this account of an incident during a trip to Georgia:

After our arrival we went up to the town of Savanna; and the same evening I went to a friend's house to lodge, whose name was Mosa, a black man. We were very happy at meeting each other; and after supper we had a light till it was between nine and

ten o'clock at night. About that time the watch
or patrol came by; and, discerning a light in the
house, they knocked at the door: we opened it;
and they came in and sat down, and drank some
punch with us: they also begged some limes of me,
as they understood I had some, which I readily
gave them. A little after this they told me I must go
to the watch-house with them: this surprised me a
good deal, after our kindness to them, and I asked
them, Why so? They said that all negroes who had
light in their house after nine o'clock were to be
taken into custody, and either pay some dollars or
be flogged.[227]

The next morning, Equiano saw a man and a woman
flogged by these "ruffians" and was only saved when "an
honest and worthy" man he sent for came to his assis-
tance. On another day, around the same town, two white
men sought to kidnap him to sell as a slave.

As soon as these men accosted me, one of them said
to the other, "This is the very fellow we are looking
for that you lost;" and the other swore immediately
that I was the identical person. On this they made
up to me, and were about to handle me; but I told
them to be still and keep off; for I had seen those
kind of tricks played upon other free blacks, and
they must not think to serve me so. At this they
paused a little, and one said to the other – it will not
do; and the other answered that I talked too good
English. I replied, I believed I did; and I had also
with me a revengeful stick equal to the occasion;

and my mind was likewise good. Happily however it was not used; and, after we had talked together a little in this manner, the rogues left me.[228]

When he decided to leave the Caribbean islands for England, he had some difficulties getting back from his Captain some money he had lent him. Equiano needed the money to pay for his journey to England:

> This I told him; but when I applied for it, though I urged the necessity of my occasion, I met with so much shuffling from him, that I began at last to be afraid of losing my money, as I could not recover it by law: for I have already mentioned, that through-out the West Indies no black man's testimony is admitted, on any occasion, against any white person whatever; and therefore my own oath would have been of no use.[229]

When he finally got his money, he tried to board a boat but ran into another problem. Every black man intending to leave the islands was required to advertise that intention publicly, to ensure they were not escaping form a white owner.

> The captain and others would not take me on board until I should advertise myself, and give notice of my going off the island. I told them of my haste to be in Montserrat, and that the time then would not admit of advertising, it being late in the evening, and the captain about to sail; but he insisted it was necessary, and other wise he said he would not take me. This reduced me to great perplexity; for if I

should be compelled to submit to this degrading necessity, which every black freeman is under, of advertising himself like a slave, when he leaves an island, and which I thought a gross imposition upon any freeman.[230]

Luckily, Equiano was able to find in a few minutes "some gentlemen of Montserrat" who "satisfied" the Captain that Equiano was a free man.

Equiano describes many acts of degradation and wickedness to himself and other black people. Many of these he clearly means to challenge not only the reader's sense of human dignity, but, also their sense of right and wrong. In one of his reflections on the treatment of slaves, he writes:

Why do you use those instruments of torture? Are they fit to be applied by one rational being to another? And are ye not struck with shame and mortification, to see the partakers of your nature reduced so low?[231]

Elsewhere he questions the common practice of separating African slaves from their relatives to sell them to different masters. Equiano believed this was unnecessarily cruel as it was on top of all the slaves had already lost and all the pain of their slavery:

Is it not enough that we are torn from our country and friends to toil for your luxury and lust of gain? Must every tender feeling be likewise sacrificed to your avarice? Are the dearest friends and relatives, now rendered more dear by their separation from their kindred [in Africa], still to be parted from each other, and thus prevented from cheering the gloom of slavery with the small comfort of being together and mingling their sufferings and sorrows? Why are parents to lose their children, brothers their sisters, or husbands their wives? Surely this is a new refinement in cruelty...[232]

In conclusion, we can say that there are clear evidence in Equiano's writing about how he understood the human being. His writing shows that he saw black and white people as being part of the same human race. This is a point many people today would take as a given, but in Equiano's day, some people believed black people were part of a sub-human race, between human beings and animals. Equiano also believed that there is a dignity that should be accorded to all human beings simply for being human. Whenever any human being, white or black, is treated in an undignified manner, all human beings suffer, because the value of what it means to be human would have been lowered.

Cugoano the Visionary

Of the four, Cugoano gives the most explicit description of an understanding of humanity in his book. This is, mainly, because his book was written as a contribution to a debate about slavery, and the nature of human beings was a central part of that debate. The influence of Christianity on his understanding is also much more explicit. In accordance with the book of Genesis, he believed that human beings were created in the image of God:

The whole law of God is founded upon love, and the two grand branches of it are these: *Thou shalt love the Lord thy God with all thy heart and with all thy soul, and thou shalt love thy neighbour as thyself.* And so it was when man was first created and made: they were created male and female, and pronounced to be in the image of God, and, as his representative, to have dominion over the lower creation: and their Maker, who is love, and the intellectual Father of Spirits, blessed them, and commanded them to arise in a bond of union of nature and of blood, each being a brother and a sister together, and each the lover and the loved of one another.[233]

Cugoano's point that human beings were made in the image of God, which is a reference to Gen 1:27, is a well known teaching within Christianity. What is less common is his view that the image in question is not a physical image or a spiritual image (however that might be understood), but the image of a loving being. Because God is love, God has created human beings to love. Those who enslave others, in this understanding, are working against God's purposes:

Those who go on to injure, ensnare, oppress, and enslave their fellow-creatures, manifest their hatred to men, and maintain their own infamous dignity and vassalage, as the servants of sin and the devil.[234]

Looking at human beings from the point of view of the creation story in Genesis, Cugoano argues that all human beings are part of one family. A good man, he writes:

> Looks up to his God and Father as his only sovereign; and he looks around on his fellow men as his brethren and friends; and in every situation and case, however mean and contemptible they may seem, he endeavours to do them good: and should he meet with one in the desert, whom he never saw before, he would hail him my brother! My sister! My friend! How fare it with thee? And if he can do any of them any good it would gladden every nerve of his soul.[235]

Since, for Cugoano, it is the tendency to love that is the main area of resemblance between God and human beings, he believed that physical features, such as complexion, has no significance in that respect. They can be attributed to climate and customs:

> As all the present inhabitants of the world sprang from the family of Noah, and were then all of one complexion, there is no doubt, but the difference which we now find, took its rife very rapidly after they became dispersed and settled on the different parts of the globe.[236]

What cannot be attributed to climate and custom must be the handwork of God, he writes. But this is nothing extraordinary, since even children from the same family sometimes have different complexion:

Therefore, as we find the distribution of the human species inhabiting the barren, as well as the most fruitful parts of the earth, and the cold as well as the most hot, differing from one another in complexion according to their situation; it may be reasonably, as well as religiously, inferred, that He who placed them in their various situations, hath extended equally his care and protection to all; and from thence, that it becometh unlawful to counteract his benignity, by reducing others of different complexion to underserved bondage.[237]

Another important theme in Cugoano's understanding of the human being is that of equality. He believed that all human beings were equal because they were equal in God's eyes:

The life of a black man is of as much regard in the sight of God, as the life of any other man; though we have been sold as a carnage to the market, and as a prey to profligate wicked men, to torture and lash us as they please, and as their caprice may think fit, to murder us at discretion.[238]

They are, also, equally entitled to God's mercies and blessings:

As we find that the difference of colour among men is only incidental, and equally natural to all, and agreeable to the place of their habitation; and that if nothing else be different or contrary among them, but that of features and complexion, in that respect, they are all equally alike entitled to the enjoyment of every mercy and blessing of God.[239]

He believed that only wickedness and ignorance could make people think that treating a black man badly is less serious than maltreating people of other colour:

Nothing but ignorance, and the dreams of a vitiated imagination, arising from the general countenance given to the evil practice of wicked men, to strengthen their hands in wickedness, could ever make any person to fancy otherwise, or ever to think that the stealing, kidnapping, enslaving, persecuting or killing a black man, is in any way and manner less criminal, than the same evil treatment of any other man of another complexion.[240]

Cugoano not only based his understanding of humanity on the Bible and the Christian religion but, was knowledgeable enough to attack those who were using the Bible to justify slavery. Some supporters of slavery were arguing at the time that slavery was allowed in the Bible under the laws of Moses. Cugoano responded by first noting that these were people who did not themselves believe in the Bible.

Those who do not believe the scriptures to be a Divine revelation, cannot, consistently with themselves, make the law of Moses... [a] reason that one class of men should enslave another.[241]

Then he argued that, in any case, what really matters is whether they think one group of people should enslave another:

In that respect, all that they have to enquire into should be, whether it be right, or wrong, that any part of the human species should enslave another; and when that is the case, the Africans, though not so learned, are just as wise as the Europeans; and when the matter is left to human wisdom, they are both liable to err.[242]

He also challenged British people with this application of reciprocity. He asked how they would feel if Africans came to their shores and kidnapped their sons and daughters. "You would certainly think that those African pirates were justly deserving of any punishment that could be put upon them".[243] He also pointed out that there was no slave holder that "would like to have himself enslaved, and to be treated as a dog, and sold like a beast."[244]

A third aspect of Cugoano's understanding of humanity is the sense of human dignity. Although this does not get the same emphasis it gets in Equiano's writing, it is nonetheless, an important part of his whole picture. He writes, in response to those who defend slavery on the account that the Africans who are enslaved acquire knowledge during their slavery:

> The argument is false; there can be no ignorance, dispersion, or unsociableness so found among them, which can be made better by bringing them away to a state of a degree equal to that of a cow or a horse.
>
> But let their ignorance in some things… be what it will, it is not the intention of those who bring them away to make them better by it; nor is the

design of slave-holders of any other intention, but that they may serve them as a kind of engines and beast of burdens; that their own ease and profit may be advanced, by a set of poor helpless men and women whom they despise and rank with brutes, and keep them in perpetual slavery, both themselves and children, and merciful death is the only release from their toil.[245]

In other word, no amount of ignorance on the part of Africans can justify enslaving them and treating them like animals. In any case, he argues, it is not the intention of those who take them into slavery to enlighten them. Their intention is to exploit the Africans for their own profit, with the result that to many Africans death becomes a "merciful" release. Cugoano's reference to animals is an indication of his belief that human beings should be treated with dignity simply for being human beings. His point about death also means that for him there is a level of degradation of human beings at which life become worthless.

In one section, Cugoano considers some of the arguments put forward by the supporters of slavery:

Should they say, that their fathers were thieves and connivers with ensnarers of men, and that they have been brought up to the iniquitous practice of slavery and oppression of their fellow creature, and they cannot live without carrying it on, and making their gain by the unlawful merchandize and cruel slavery of men, what is that to us, and where will it justify them?[246]

He also considers the argument of those who say that slavery is not really bad to black people because some free blacks in the West Indies suffer more hardship:

> ...some will be saying, that the Black people, who are free in the West Indies, are more miserable than the slaves; - and well they may; for while they can get their work and drudgery done for nothing, it is not likely that they will employ those whom they must pay for their labour.[247]

Cugoano's point here is that, if free black people in the West Indies are poor, it is still because of slavery, in that so long as white people can get labour for nothing from slaves, they will not employ free black people who they would have to pay for their labour. Cugoano dismisses this search for an honourable explanation for slavery:

> Whatever necessity the enslavers of men may plead for their iniquitous practice of slavery, and the various advantages which they get by it, can only evidence their own injustice and dishonesty. A man that is truly honest, fears nothing so much as the very imputation of justice; but those men who dare not face the consequence of acting uprightly in every case are detestable cowards, unworthy the name of men.[248]

By the phrase "unworthy the name of men" Cugoano shows that "men" (by which he probably means "human beings") is a description which demands a certain level of behaviour. The cowardly dereliction of the responsibilities that naturally fall on human beings can jeopardize a group's entitlement to called "men".

Cugoano's belief that human being are deserving of dignity can be seen in the many references he makes to animal-like treatment that slaves receive. Responding to the argument by supporter of slavery, that Africans are not capable of receiving knowledge and are, therefore, only fit for slavery, Cugoano writes:

> When I meet with those who make no scruples to deal with the human species, as with the beasts of the earth, I must think them not only brutish, but wicked and base; and that their aspersions are insidious and false: And if such men can boast of greater degree of knowledge, than any African is entitled to, I shall let them enjoy all the advantages of it unenvied, as I fear it consists only in a greater share of infidelity, and that of a blacker kind than only skin deep.[249]

Cugoano was also the one out of the four Africans who wrote the most about the rights of the slaves as human beings, but this will be considered in the next chapter. For now, one can conclude that the writing of Ottobah Cugoano shows how he understood humanity. His understanding is securely rooted in his Christian faith. He believed that human beings are made in the image of God. The point of resemblance for him was the tendency to love, so he deduced that human beings are by nature creatures that want to love. He believed, following the Biblical story of Adam and Eve, that all human beings, white and black, originate from the same father and mother. This automatically makes them brothers and sisters. A key idea for Cugoano is that of equality and he approached this from a number of angles. For example, he argued that all people, black or white, have equal regard in the sight of God and equally disposed to be blessed by God. He also dismissed skin colour, commonly used at the time to categorise human beings, as being the product of climate. He believed strongly in the dignity of the human species, and often made this point by arguing that human beings should not be treated like animals.

Concluding Remarks

As we have done in previous chapters, we will end by imagining that these four Africans were making a joint presentation to us about their understanding of humanity. Sancho would start his presentation by saying that for him human life for its own sake and human beings in themselves are not worth much. What gives value to life is the good one can do to other people in one's lifetime. In so doing they would be imitating the grace and mercy of God in their life. This, he would explain, was why he tried in his life to wish people well and set them on their way. It was also the reason why he liked the arts so much. He sees art as a means through which a person can make an addition to the world and give pleasure to others. This, for him, is what is wrong with the world. People are too ready to blame and too reluctant to praise. But it is in fact the praising and blessing of others that the world needs more of and it is in so doing that we give value to our own humanity.

Gronniosaw would say that he agreed with Sancho that human beings and human life do not have meaning in themselves. He would take it further by saying that human life gets not only meaning but sustenance by God. He might use the analogy of every individual having a certain amount of spiritual credit to their name, and if they paid no attention to this and spent it recklessly in sinful living, sooner or later they would run out. He would say that he has on occasion been painfully aware of his own sinfulness and worthlessness before God. On one occasion this has driven him close to the brink, but God was at hand to save him. He would say that the knowledge that he was saved from being crushed by his sense of worthlessness continues to be the basis of his faith in God today. He would end by wondering why some Christians who like him must have experienced the transformative power of God continue to live like unsaved human beings.

Equiano would start by saying that an important dimension to all this is not only what a human being could or should be, but what a human being actually is. In that sense, what he regards as important is that he, Equiano, Sancho, Gronniosaw and Cugoano; and everybody listening to or reading this are all human beings, whether or not they are generous, creative or sinful. He also believes that each one of them is automatically entitled to be treated with a certain level of dignity and respect just for being human. Approaching the matter in that way is important because that was how they might get the sense of their common humanity – that is, the sense that they are human beings together. It is that shared sense of humanity that often stops people from attacking or degrading each other. He might give the example of those people who were arguing that black people were sub-human beings during the debate for abolition in order to make it easier for them to enslave and maltreat black people. If those people had been allowed to succeed, he would say, slavery would probably still be going on today. So, he would conclude, by urging that whatever anybody might aspire for human beings let that not take them away from stating the basic humanity of everyone.

Cugoano, going fourth, would say he agreed with Equiano's point. He would point out, perhaps clutching a Bible, that there is ample support for such a view in the Bible. He would point to the Bible saying that human beings were made in the image of God and the creation story which says that all human beings come from Adam and Eve. From this he would argue that every human being shares this image of God and belongs to this one family. This, he would point out, was what supporters of slavery were getting wrong. They were suggesting that one group of humanity was superior to the other on account of complexion or other physical features. What they had not done was read their Bible properly to see that it was not the case. Every human being, he would say, was equally entitled to Gods' blessings and mercies. It is only wickedness and ignorance that would make anybody think that maltreating or killing a black person was less of a crime than maltreating or killing a white person.

CHAPTER 6:
ATTITUDE TO SLAVERY

Introduction

Slavery was a major issue in the lives of the four Africans we are looking at. Although I have tried, as much as possible, to consider the lives of the four as individuals, a brief overview of slavery is unavoidable. Sancho, Gronniosaw, Equiano and Cugoano lived a number of years of their lives as slaves, so their own slavery and the slavery of other Africans was clearly in their mind when they wrote. This was particularly the case for Equiano and Cugoano moreso than for Sancho and Gronniosaw. In this chapter, we will look at their attitude to slavery and the slave trade.

Sancho the Poet

Sancho's attitude to his own slavery can be seen from his early life. This is how Jekyll, who wrote the first account of Sancho's life, described those early days:

The extraordinary Negro, whose life I am about to write, was born A.D. 1729, on board a ship in the Slave-trade, a few days after it had quitted the coast of Guinea for the Spanish West-Indies, and at Carthagena he received from the hand of the Bishop, Baptism, and the name of Ignatius…At little more than two-years-old, his master brought him to England, and gave him to three maiden sisters, resident at Greenwich, whose prejudice had unhappily taught them that African ignorance was the only security for his obedience, and that to enlarge the mind of their slave would go near to emancipating his person. The petulance of their disposition surnamed him Sancho, from a fancied resemblance to the 'Squire of *Don Quixote*.[250]

Sancho, however, got help from a friend to the sisters, the Duke of Montagu, who lived at nearby Blackheath at the time:

The late Duke of Montagu lived on Blackheath: he accidentally saw the little Negro, and admired in him a native frankness of manner as yet unbroken by servitude, and unrefined by education – He brought him frequently home to the Duchess, indulged his turn for reading with presents of books, and strongly recommended to his mistress the duty of cultivating a genius of such apparent fertility.[251]

The trouble with the sisters persisted, though. They even threatened, on some occasions, to return Sancho to a harsh form of slavery. After the Duke died, Sancho continued to be close to his wife, the Duchess. When he could not bear the sister's ill treatment anymore, he ran away to the Duchess. But the Duchess tried to send him back to the sisters. That, Sancho found unbearable. He was through with being treated as a slave, and, as Jekyll writes, "He procured an old pistol for purposes which his father's example had suggested as familiar, and had sanctified as hereditary." In other words, he wanted to follow in his father's footsteps and commit suicide rather than be maltreated as a slave. The Duchess learnt about this and took him back.

Although Sancho did not write many letters on the subject of slavery, in the few letters in which he mentioned slavery, his view was that slavery was wrong and should be stopped. For example, in a letter to one Mr Fisher, who had sent him some anti-slavery books from America, Sancho began by describing slavery as diabolical, cruel and wicked:

> Full heartily and most cordially do I thank thee, good Mr Fisher, for your kindness in sending the books – That upon the unchristian and most diabolical usage of my brother Negroes – the illegality - the horrid wickedness of the traffic – the cruel carnage and depopulation of the human species – is painted in such strong colours – that I should think would (if duly attended to) flash conviction – and produce remorse in every enlightened and candid reader.[252]

Then he described how reading about the suffering of fellow Africans upset him, and yet made him feel thankful to the writers for highlighting the issue:

The perusal affected me more than I can express; - indeed I felt a double or mixt sensation – for while my heart was torn for the sufferings- which, for aught I know – some of my nearest kin might have undergone – my bosom, at the same time, glowed with gratitude – and praise toward the humane – the Christian - the friendly and learned Author of the most valuable book.[253]

For his anti-slavery ideas, Sancho believed the writer of the book he read was the best man in the whole American continent, I…look upon the friendly Author – as a being far superior to any great name upon your continent."[254]

Sancho also hoped that the Members of the British Parliament and the King of England would read the books, probably, in the hope that the books would turn them against the slave trade:

I could wish that every member of each house of parliament had one of these books. And if his Majesty perused one through before breakfast – though it might spoil his appetite – yet the consciousness of having it in his power to facilitate the great work [i.e. abolition of the slave trade] would give an additional sweetness to his tea.[255]

One of the books Sancho was commenting on appears to be a collection of poems by an African slave girl called Phyllis Wheatley. Phyllis's life is another sad story of its own. She was bought at about the age of seven by her mistress, the wife of a tailor in Boston, Massachusetts. Her age was, apparently, estimated by the shedding of her front tooth.[256] It quickly became clear that she was very clever. Her owner taught her to read and write and within 16 months, she was reading the Bible. She also learnt Latin at a young age and was often visited by people of high standing.[257] She started writing poems at about the age of 13. At about 19, she visited London for a month as "a kind of cultural ambassador" for the city of Boston. Upon her return to America she wrote her best known work, a collection of 39 poems published in London in 1773, called *Poems on Various Subjecst, Religious and Moral.* Peter Fryer writes this about Phyllis's visit to London:

> When Phyllis came to England in 1773, in the company of her mistress son, she was lionized.[258] The countess of Huntingdon, to whom she had dedicated her first published poem three years before, introduced her to the Earl of Dartmouth and other prominent members of London society. Her visitors included Benjamin Franklin, then agent in Europe of the North American colonies. The lord mayor of London presented her with a valuable edition of Milton's *Paradise Lost.*[259]

But all these were to change. After Phyllis's mistress died, she fell into hard times. At one point, she was selling her books door-to-door to get by. She married a man who was in and out of jail for not paying his debt. Of her three children two died and the third was often very ill. Phyllis herself died, aged only 30. Fryer describes the end of Phyllis's story with these words:

America's first black woman poet died in 1784, in a poor boarding house, 'surrounded by all the emblems of a squalid poverty'. She was hardly more than 30. Her third child survived her by just a few hours.[260]

At the time Sancho was reading Phyllis's poems, she was still alive and was still being feted by high society. That was what Sancho disapproved of. How could white society enjoy this young woman's writing so much and yet keep her under slavery. Firstly, Sancho writes, how could her master still be keeping her as a slave:

> Phyllis's poems do credit to nature – and put art – merely as art – to the blush. – it reflects nothing either to the glory or generosity of her master – if she is still his slave – except he glories in the *low vanity* of having in his wanton power a mind animated by Heaven - a genius superior to himself.[261]

Sancho marvelled at the long list of reputable names that would often have to sign to show that Phyllis's work was really hers, and wondered why they too were standing aside while Phyllis continued to live in slavery:

> The list of splendid – titled – learned names, in confirmation of her being the real authoress – alas! shows how very poor the acquisition of wealth and knowledge is – without generosity – feeling – and humanity. – These good great folk – all know - and perhaps admired – nay, praised Genius in bondage – and then, like the Priests and the Levites in sacred

writ, passed by – not one good Samaritan amongst them."[262]

To Sancho, liberty from slavery was worth much more than praise.

Another letter which gives us insight into Sancho's attitude towards slavery is a letter he wrote to one Reverend Sterne, probably in 1766. Sancho had just read something written by Sterne condemning slavery, so he wrote back to thank Sterne for addressing that issue. Sterne's words were these:

> Consider how great a part of our species – in all ages down to this – has been trod under the feet of cruel and capricious tyrants, who would neither hear their cries, nor pity their distresses. – Consider slavery – what it is – how bitter draught – and how many millions are made to drink it![263]

Sancho was very excited by Sterne's interest in this issue and urged him to write more on it for the sake of African slaves:

> Of all my favourite authors, not one has drawn a tear in favour of my miserable black brethren – excepting yourself, and the humane author of Sir George Ellison. – I think you will forgive me; - I am sure you will applaud me for beseeching you to give one half-hour's attention to slavery, as it is this day practised in our West Indies. – That subject, handled in your striking manner, would ease the yoke (perhaps) of many…[264]

And he added this in order to make clear that he was writing on behalf of his fellow Africans:

> Dear Sir, think in me you behold the uplifted hands of thousands of my brother Moors. – Grief…is eloquent; - figure to yourself their attitudes; - hear their supplicating addresses! – alas! – you cannot refuse. – Humanity must comply…[265]

Whilst what we have seen so far shows Sancho's disapproval of slavery, in truth he did not write a great deal about slavery. This could have been due to the fact that Sancho's friends were mostly white people and he was observing sensitivities in relating with them. It might also explain some of his deprecatory remarks about black people or his own blackness. Take for example, his comments regarding a riot in central London in 1779, arising out of a campaign against granting Roman Catholics some rights. It was described as the worst riot in England in the 18th century. Hundreds of people were killed and many public buildings burnt down. Sancho, reporting this to a friend, writes:

> Dear and most respectable sir
>   In the midst of the most cruel and ridiculous confusion, I am now set down to give you a very imperfect sketch of the maddest people that the maddest times were ever plagued with. – The public prints have informed you (without doubt) of last Friday's transactions; - the insanity of Lord George Gordon [the riot leader], and the worse than Negro barbar-

ity of the populace, - the burnings and devastations
of each night you will also see in the prints[266].

Sancho's description of the actions of the rioters as
"worse than Negro barbarity" could be seen as an associa-
tion of black people with barbarism.

Another negative portrayal of Africa can be seen in
a letter of recommendation Sancho wrote to a family he
knew on behalf of another black man He writes:

> Dear Sir
>
> If I knew a better man than yourself – you wou'd
> not have had this application – which is in behalf of
> a merry – chirping – white tooth'd – clean – tight
> – and light little fellow; - with a woolly pate - and
> face as dark as your humble; - Guney-born, and
> French-bred – the sulky gloom of Africa dispelled
> by Gallic vivacity – and that softened again with
> English sedateness – a rare fellow![267]

Sancho's point appears to be that the effect of slavery, which he termed "the sulky gloom of Africa", has
been removed by the man's time in France and England.
In parts of the book, Sancho laughs at himself. He calls
himself "a poor Blacky grocer", "a poor, thick-lipped son
of Afric" and a fat man with "a black face into the bar-
gain".

These two sides make Sancho a complex character.
In considering his negative concepts of Africa, it is worth
bearing in mind that unlike the other three Africans we
are looking at, he was not born in Africa. He had not
lived in Africa and so had no first hand knowledge of life

in Africa. The portrayals of Africa he saw around him as he grew up among white people would have been pre-dominantly negative. He was also a man who lived all of his life in white English households. Fryer termed him "a black English man", not as a criticism but as a simple statement of fact.

Another point that has been made about Sancho is that what we see of him might be a posture that he adopted to life in order to survive. He sometimes writes as if he was laughing at himself for being black. But from time to time he shows the frustration and anger bub-bling under the surface. One such occasion was when young Jack Wingrave, a family friend, who was in India wrote back home, complaining about the behaviour of the natives. Sancho gave the poor fellow a piece of his mind:

> My good friend, you should remember from whom they learnt those vices from…I say it is with reluc-tance that I must observe your countries conduct has been uniformly wicked in the East – West-Indies – and even on the coast of Guinea…In Africa, the poor wretched natives – blessed with the most fertile and luxuriant soil – are rendered so much the more miserable for what Providence meant as a blessing: - the Christian' abominable Traffic for slaves – and the horrid cruelty and treachery of the petty kings - encouraged by their Christian customers – who carry them strong liquors, to enflame their national madness – and powder and bad fire-arms, to fur-nish them with the hellish means of killing and kidnapping.[268]

In conclusion, Sancho's early life shows he was prepared to fight against servitude and enslavement. He ran away from three sisters who were maltreating him and would have killed himself rather than returning to the bad treatment he was receiving. His published collection does not have many letters on the subject of slavery. What it does have shows his strong disapproval for slavery. For example, he wrote to Reverend Sterne, thanking him for his writing against slavery and urging him to write more. He also wrote to one Mr Fisher thanking him for some anti-slavery books and hoping that politicians and the king would read them to turn them against the slave trade. Sancho was not, however, always positive about black people or his own blackness. But such might be expected of a person who, for a start, was not actually born in Africa and did not experience African life firsthand, but also lived most of his life in English households at least a decade before the fight for abolition gathered pace. The indication is that underneath the surface of this "black Englishman" was a man who believed that the slavery of Africans was wrong.

Gronniosaw the Noble

Of the four Africans we are looking at, Ukawsaw Gronniosaw was the most resigned to his enslavement. This resignation sometimes comes across as a positive attitude towards slavery. It is, in fact, difficult to find a point in his story where he described slavery as something wrong. He often paints his white slave masters in good light, seeing the best of motives in their actions. He said this about his first master, the Dutch captain of a ship, who bought him in the West African coast:

> When I left my dear mother, I had a large quantity of gold about me, as is the custom of our country, it was made into rings, and they were linked into one another, and formed into a kind of chain, and so put round my neck, and arms and legs, and a large piece hanging at one ear, almost in the shape of a pear. I found all this troublesome, and was glad when my new master took it from me. I was now washed, and clothed in the Dutch or English manner. My master grew very fond of me, and I loved him exceedingly; I watched every look, was always ready when he wanted me, and endeavoured to convince him, by every action, that my only pleasure was to serve him well.[269]

It does not seem to have occurred to Gronniosaw that his master might have been taking his gold rings for himself. He was, obviously, only a young teenager when this happened, and so might not have been capable of such thoughts. But narrating the incident at sixty years of age, there was still no hint of such thinking.

The same tone of voice can be detected as Gronniosaw narrates how the Dutch captain sold him to another man:

> I was exceedingly sea-sick at first; but when I became more accustomed to the sea, it wore off. My master's ship was bound for Barbados. When he came there, he thought fit to speak of me to several gentlemen

of his acquaintance, and one of them expressed a particular desire to see me. He had a great mind to buy me; but the Captain could not immediately be prevailed on to part with me; but however, as the gentleman seemed very solicitous, he at length let me go, and I was sold for fifty dollars (*four and sixpenny piece in English*).[270]

Most people in Gronniosaw's situation would probably have seen what was going on between his master and the potential buyer as a haggling process. Perhaps, as happens with most sales, the seller was asking for more money than the buyer was initially willing to pay, and they were negotiating a price. In Gronniosaw's presentation, it would appear his master wanted to hold on to him because he liked him very much. This is, of course, is possible, but it would raise the question about why his master went to speak to "several gentlemen of his acquaintance" about Gronniosaw when they arrived, other than that he was seeking for a buyer.

Gronniosaw's second master was, according to Gronniosaw, equally good:

> My new master's name was Vanhorn, a young gentleman; his home was in New-England, in the city of New York, to which place he took me with him. He dressed me in his livery, and was very good to me. My chief business was to wait at table and tea, and clean knives, and I had a very easy place.[271]

When Gronniosaw was being sold by Vanhorn to his third master Mr Freelandhouse, there was yet another exchange, which from Gronniosaw's description, was of two people both of whom wanted him. It all began when Gronniosaw said something which displeased his mistress:

> My mistress was not angry with me, but rather diverted with my simplicity, and by way of talk, she repeated what I had said to many of her acquaintance that visited her; among the rest Mr Freelandhouse, a very gracious good Minister, heard it, and he took a great deal of notice of me, and desired my master to part with me to him. He would not hear of it at first, but being greatly persuaded, he let me go, and Mr Freelandhouse gave fifty pounds for me.[272]

The difficulty of Gronniosaw's situation has to be appreciated. He was older than the other three Africans we are looking at. He was born about or before 1710, 19 years before Sancho, 35 years before Equiano and 47 years before Cugoano. He lived at an earlier stage of the slavery era than the rest. Even after he got his freedom, the situation would not have been much different. His status as a fee black man would have been quite a precarious one. All it might have taken was one wrong turn and he could have found himself pushed back into slavery. So he would have been in a very weak position to fight for himself. Secondly, his story was not written by himself. He dictated it to somebody described as a "young lady of Leominster". This lady was probably a white woman and that fact could have made Gronniosaw avoid denouncing white people or even slavery.

For whatever reason, Gronniosaw's story is that of a man who appears to be resigned with his place as a slave. Take for example, his attitude to education. Unlike Sancho, whose owners tried hard to keep him ignorant in order to control him while he worked hard to thwart their plan and taught himself to read and write, Gronniosaw would not go to school when he was sent by his master, Mr Freelandhouse:

> My dear kind master grew fond of me, as was his lady; she put me to school, but I was uneasy at that, and did not like to go; but my master and mistress requested me to learn in the gentlest terms, and persuaded me to attend my school without any anger at all; that, at last, I came to like it better, and learnt to read pretty well.[273]

Gronniosaw got his freedom when his master, Mr Freelandhouse, died. In his will, Mr Freelandhouse left for Gronniosaw ten pounds and his freedom. But Gronniosaw did not show the kind of relief one might expect at the news of getting their freedom:

> I found that if he [Mr Freelandhouse] had lived, it was his intention to take me with him to Holland, as he had often mentioned me to some friends of his there, that were desirous to see me: but I chose to continue with my mistress, who was as good to me as if she had been my mother.[274]

Not only did Gronniosaw stay with his mistress, but when she died, he stayed on with the couple's children.

Sometime later, after Gronniosaw had moved from New York to London, he did, in fact, go to Holland, somewhat in honour of his former master, Mr Freelandhouse:

> After I had been in London about six weeks, I was recommended to the notice of some of my late master Mr Freelandhouse's acquaintance, who had heard him speak frequently of me. I was much persuaded by them to go to Holland. My master lived there before he bought me and used to speak of me so respectfully among his friends there, that it raised in them a curiosity to see me; particularly the gentlemen engaged in the ministry, who expressed a desire to hear my experience and examine me.[275]

In Holland, Gronniosaw spoke to a group of 38 ministers every Thursday for seven weeks. He described how pleased he was for this opportunity to tell his story. The impression one can get, however, from his story is of one still not quite sure what to do with his freedom. It is as though he was still trying to please his dead master, Mr Freelandhouse.

Gronniosaw's strong loyalty towards his master was, apparently, common among domestic slaves. This would have been an important strategy for coping with life in slavery. Such a coping strategy probably also affected his attitude to black people generally. His story certainly shows that he was conscious of his blackness and its effect on people and on him. After a disappointing event one day, he described how he felt that "everybody and everything despised me because I was black."[276] Gronniosaw might have developed a negative attitude towards Africa

and blackness as a way of coping with other people's attitude towards him. For example, when he was told about
God, he thought to himself how this was going to make
him wiser than his people back in Africa:

> He told me that God was a Great and Good Spirit,
> that He created all the world, and every person and
> thing, in Ethiopia, Africa and America, and every
> where. I was delighted when I heard this: There, says
> I, I always thought so when I lived at home! Now if
> I had wings like an eagle, I would fly to tell my dear
> mother that God is greater than the sun, moon, and
> stars; and that they were made by Him… I thought
> now if I could but go home, I should be wiser than
> all my country folks, my grandfather, or father, or
> mother, or any of them.[277]

This negative attitude towards being black can also be
seen in another incident which concerns Gronniosaw con-
ception of the Devil. The issue arose because Gronniosaw
was seen swearing at another servant:

> One day I had just cleaned the knives for dinner,
> when one of the maids took one to cut bread and
> butter with; I was very angry with her, and imme-
> diately called upon God to damn her; when this
> old black man told me I must not say so. I asked
> him why? He replied that there was a wicked man
> called the Devil, who lived in hell, and would take
> all who said these words, and put them into the fire
> and burn them. This terrified me greatly, and I was
> entirely broke off swearing.[278]

Soon after this, Gronniosaw caught his mistress swearing and gave her the same warning he had received:

> ...as I was placing the china for tea, my mistress came into the room just as the maid had been clearing it; the girl had unfortunately sprinkled the wainscot with the mop, at which my mistress was very angry, the girl very foolishly answered her again, which made her worse, and she called upon God to damn her. I was vastly concerned to hear this, as she was a fine young lady, and very good to me... "Madam, says I, you must not say so." Why, says she? Because there is a black man called the Devil that lives in hell, and he will put you into the fire and burn you, and I shall be very sorry for that. Who told you this, replied my lady? Old Ned, says I. Very well, was all her answer.[279]

According to Gronniosaw, Old Ned told him "there was a *wicked* man called the Devil", but when Gronniosaw was talking to his mistress, he said, "there is a *black* man called the Devil". This might be a simple mistake in the narration. Or it could be an indication of how Gronniosaw has been conditioned by his enslavement to associate black people with negative things.

In conclusion, Gronniosaw's story shows that he was a man that was resigned to his status as a slave. When he was a slave, he often appeared much more concerned about getting good slave masters than about becoming free. Even after he got his freedom, he appeared to live in the shadow of his former master. This is understandable because at the time he lived in Britain, slavery was a much more acceptable part of life and Gronniosaw did not have a leg to stand on. Even after they became legally free, the life of a black person was still very precarious. There was a constant threat of being kidnapped and resold into harsh slavery and they had very little rights under the law. Gronniosaw's way of surviving in this social climate was by relying on God and the goodwill of the white people around him.

Equiano the Activist

Equiano has been described as "the most remarkable" of the Africans who lived in Britain during the era of slavery. This is mainly because of the stand he took against the slave trade. His book, the *Interesting Narrative*, from which we have been extracting his views on different subjects, was written, by his own admission, with the goal of swaying British opinion on slavery and the slave trade. We will now look at what he said at different points in his life about slavery and the slave trade.

His life in slavery began when he and his sister were kidnapped in his African village one day, when all the adults in his compound had gone out:

> Two men and a woman got over our walls, and in a moment seized us both, and, without giving us time to cry out, or make resistance, they stopped our mouths, and ran off with us into the nearest wood.[280]

Equiano, who was about 11 at the time, was sold on from merchant to merchant until he came to the coast:

The first object which saluted my eyes when I arrived on the coast was the sea, and a slave ship, which was then riding at anchor, and waiting for its cargo. These filled me with astonishment, which was soon converted into terror when I was carried on board. I was immediately handled and tossed up to see if I were sound by some of the crew; and I was now persuaded that I had gotten into a world of bad spirits, and that they were going to kill me. The complexion too differing so much from ours, their long hair, and the language they spoke, (which was very different from any I had ever heard) united to confirm me in this belief. Indeed such were the horrors of my views and fears at the moment, that, if ten thousand worlds had been my own, I would have freely parted with them all to have exchanged my condition with that of the meanest slave in my own country.[281]

His fears were deepened by other black people he saw being held there:

When I looked round the ship too and saw a large furnace of copper boiling, and a multitude of black people of every description chained together, every one of their countenances expressing dejection and sorrow, I no longer doubted of my fate; and, quite overpowered with horror and anguish, I fell motion-less on the deck and fainted.[282]

He came round to observe the black people who brought him being paid by the white slave merchants:

When I recovered a little I found some black people about me, who I believe were some of those who brought me on board; and had been receiving their pay… Soon after this the blacks who brought me on board went off, and left me abandoned to despair.[283]

Equiano's life as a slave is indeed an "interesting narrative". Unlike the other three whose times in slavery were spent as household servants, Equiano spent most of his time on the sea. His first master was a British naval officer called Michael Pascal. Equiano served him aboard a British battle ship, where he leant some of the ships manoeuvres and made several times to fire the guns.[284] After Michael Pascal sold him unexpectedly, he worked on different trading boats mainly in the Caribbean islands.

Equiano's attitude towards his enslavement appears to be characterised by a commitment to give honest service to whoever was his master, while working hard towards his own freedom. He looked forward to the day he would be free, and even regarded that freedom more important than life itself. Equiano makes that point one day when a white man who had bought goods off him returned to their ship the following day without the goods, and started to demand his money back:

I refused to give it; and, not seeing my captain on board, he began the common pranks with me; and swore he would even break open my chest and take my money. I therefore expected, as my captain was absent, that he would be as good as his word: and he was just proceeding to strike me, when fortunately a

British seaman on board, whose heart had not been debauched by a West India climate [i.e. the cruel slavery of the West Indies] interposed and prevented him. But had the cruel man struck me I certainly should have defended myself at the hazard of my life; for what is life to a man thus oppressed?[285]

He made a similar point regarding his dealings with the captain of the ship he was working on that:

Whenever he treated me waspishly I used plainly to tell him my mind, and that I would die before I would be imposed on as other negroes were, and that to me life had lost its relish when liberty was gone. This I said although I foresaw my then well-being or future hope of freedom (humanly speaking) depended on this man. However, as he could not bear the thoughts of my not sailing with him, he always became mild on my threats. I therefore continued with him; and, from my great attention to his orders and his business, I gained him credit, and through his kindness to me I at last procured my liberty.[286]

It was this captain that Equiano took along with him when he had made enough money to buy his freedom, to see his master.

When we had unladen the vessel, and I had sold my venture, finding myself master of about forty-seven pounds, I consulted my true friend, the Captain, how I should proceed in offering my master the money for my freedom. He told me to come on a certain morning when he and my master would be at breakfast together. Accordingly, on that morning I went, and met the Captain there, as he had appointed. When I went in I made my obeisance to my master, and with my money in my hand, and many fears in heart, I prayed him to be as good as his offer to me, when he was pleased to promise me my freedom as soon as I could purchase it.[287]

Equiano's master was reluctant to allow him to buy himself, asking how he had made 40 pounds so quickly. However, with the Captain assuring him that Equiano had made the money honestly, he allowed this to happen:

> My master then said, he would not be worse than his promise; and, taking the money, told me to go to the Secretary at the Registry Office, and get my manumission drawn up. These words of my master were like a voice from heaven to me: in an instant all my trepidation was turned into unutterable bliss; and I most reverently bowed myself with gratitude, unable to express my feelings, but by the over-flowing of my eyes, while my true and worthy friend, the Captain, congratulated us both with a peculiar degree of heart-felt pleasure.[288]

He was thus the only one of the four about whom we know for sure that his freedom was not "given" to him by his master. He had worked hard to earn enough money on the side during his trading trips for his master in order to buy his freedom. Even though he had opportunities to escape, he did not use them, preferring instead to buy his freedom honestly.

He did continue to face challenges even as a free man, but he continued to rise up to them. Take for example, these three incidents which took place in Georgia. The first concerns another black man:

> One evening a slave belonging to Mr Read, a merchant of Savannah, came near our vessel, and began to use me very ill. I entreated him, with all the patience I was master of, to desist, as I knew there was little or no law for a free negro here; but the fellow, instead of taking my advice, persevered in his insults, and even struck me. At this I lost all temper, and I fell on him and beat him soundly.[289]

The black man's master came aboard the ship Equiano was based in requesting that he come ashore to be flogged all around the town, for beating up his negro slave, but Equiano's Captain protected him.

Equiano's life and the life of other slaves and even free black people that he witnessed convinced him that slavery was wrong. He made his way to England shortly after buying his freedom and after more years as a trader, settled in London and spent the rest of his life fighting slavery and the slave trade. He emphasised the justice of God and the dignity of human beings as part of that fight. He wrote and said much more beside, some of which we will now describe.

One of Equiano's arguments was that slavery was morally wrong. He asked British people, to whom his book was directed, why they were allowing torture instruments to be used on people, "Are they fit to be applied by one rational being to another?" he asked. He told the story of a black man who was hanged and when he was half-dead, he was burnt for trying to poison his overseer. Equiano pointed out that the man was only doing what was natural for a person to do, that is, to pursue their freedom.

> Thus by repeated cruelties are the wretched first urged to despair, and then murdered, because they still retain so much of human nature about them as to wish to put an end to their misery, and retaliate on their tyrants![290]

The sheer number of people who were dying in slavery was another reason he gave why slavery was wrong. In the islands, 20,000 new negroes were needed annually just to replace those who had died.

He believed that slavery was not the most economic way of getting labour because the Africans were so badly used that they died quickly.

> Their huts, which ought to be well covered, and the place dry where they take their little repose, are often open sheds, built in damp places; so that, when the poor creatures return tired from the toils of the field, they contract many disorders, from being exposed to the damp air in this uncomfortable state, while they are heated, and their pores are open. This neglect certainly conspires with many others to cause a decrease in the birth as well as in the lives of the grown negroes.[291]

Much of the bad treatment is down to the overseers, whom Equiano describes as:

> …human butchers, who cut and mangle the slaves in a shocking manner on the most trifling occasions, and altogether treat them in every respect like brutes. They pay no regard to the situation of pregnant women, nor the least attention to the lodging of the field negroes.[292]

Those plantations where the overseers treated slaves well, giving them rest appropriately, had the slaves working for them for longer and the slaves themselves were happier.

In his view, however, it was not really the overseers or slave dealers that should be blamed for the wickedness he had described, but the whole industry of slavery and the slave trade. It was the buying and selling of human beings and the legal practice of using them as forced labour that was turning these men into such horrible people.

> Such a tendency has the slave-trade to debauch men's mind, and harden them to every feeling of humanity! For I will not suppose that the dealers in slaves are born worse than other men – No; it is the fatality of his mistaken avarice [i.e. the slave trade] that it corrupts the milk of human kindness and turns it into gall. And, had the pursuits of those men been different, they might have been as generous, as tender-hearted and just, as they are unfeeling, rapacious and cruel.[293]

And he adds regarding slavery:

Surely this traffic cannot be good, which spread like a pestilence, and taints what it touches! which violates that first natural right of mankind, equality and independence, and gives one man a dominion over his fellows which God could never intend! For it raises the owner to a state as far above man as it depresses the slave below it; and, with all the presumption of human pride, sets a distinction between them, immeasurable in extent, and endless in duration![294]

He answered white people who were arguing that Africans should be used as slaves because they are inferior to whites by asking them whether their own ancestors who were less civilised than they were inferior to them, "...did nature make them inferior to their sons? And should they have been made slaves?"[295] He then pointed out that the Africans they saw were those living under slavery, which meant that they have never really witnesseded what Africans were like outside of that circumstance:

When you make men slaves you deprive them of half their virtue, you set them in your own conduct an example of fraud, rapine, and cruelty, and compel them to live with you in a state of war; and yet you complain that they are not honest or faithful! You stupefy them with stripes, and think it necessary to keep them in a state of ignorance; and yet you assert that they are incapable of learning.[296]

These and other arguments Equiano set out in his book, *Interesting Narrative*, which he travelled all over

Britain and Ireland to promote. His book was a bestseller. It struck a chord among the British population
and is still regarded as a major contribution to the fight
for abolition. For example, the publication is listed by the
historian James Walvin among the landmark events on
the road to abolition.[297] The book was not his only contribution. He also engaged many public supporters of the
slave trade in London newspapers and worked closely with
both white and black abolitionists such as Cugoano and
Sharp. He, along with other free black men in England,
formed a group called the Sons of Africa who wrote to
the members of the British parliament and to white abolitionists to encourage them. He also worked closely with
the Quakers, who were the first notable opposition to the
slave trade. His book contains an address of thanks he
gave to the Quakers in October 1785 at Lombard street,
London, accompanied by other Africans.

When an expedition was planned by the government
to send some Africans back to Sierra Leone, Equiano was
persuaded by other abolitionists to accept an appointment
by the government as the Commissary. This meant he
was the official representative of the interest of the black
people being shipped back to Africa. When the contrac-
tor failed to pass on provisions to the black people from
the government, Equiano petitioned to the authorities
but found even though official investigation showed he
was right, it was he that lost his position because he was a
black man. His contribution to the abolition project ranks
with those of Sharp, Clarkson and Wilberforce. At the
end of his book he sums up his hope in these words:

Tortures, murder and every other imaginable barbarity and iniquity, are practised upon the poor
slaves with impunity. I hope the slave trade will be
abolished. I pray it may be an event at hand.[298]

In conclusion, Equiano's life story is that of a person
who used all within his power to fight against slavery and
the slave trade. His life during his own slavery shows a
person who would not allow himself to be overwhelmed
by his enslavement. He maintained a longing for freedom
and worked hard towards it. He was the only one of the
four we are looking at who, as far as we know, bought his
own freedom himself. After he did this, he spent most
of his time campaigning for the abolition of slaves. He
argued among other things that God was against slavery,
that it was undermining human dignity and that it was
not even economical. His book, *Interesting Narrative*, was
a major contribution to the fight for abolition and Equiano
himself was a key figure in Britain and Ireland, working
closely with both white and black abolitionists. As the
leader of Britain's black community, Equiano's impact on
the cause of abolition ranks among the highest.

Cugoano the Visionary

Cugoano's life in slavery, like Equiano's, began when he
was kidnapped from his Fante village in modern day
Ghana. His kidnappers, who he described as "several great
ruffians", had matchets and a gun and took him with
other boys from the wood where they were playing and
made their way to the coast. This trip took some days

and Cugoano gave this description of what he saw when
they arrived:

> After I was ordered out, the horrors I soon saw
> and felt, cannot be well described; I saw many of
> my miserable countrymen chained two and two,
> some hand-cuffed, and some with their hands tied
> behind. We were conducted along by a guard, and
> when we arrived at the castle, I asked my guide what
> I was brought there for, he told me to learn the ways
> of the *browfow*, that is the white faced people…
> I was soon conducted to a prison, for three days,
> where I heard the groans and cries of many, and saw
> some of my fellow-captives.[299]

Cugoano also describes the scene when the slaves were
being taken to board the ship:

> When a vessel arrived to conduct us away to the
> ship, it was a most horrible scene; there was noth-
> ing to be heard but rattling of chains, smacking of
> whips, and the groans and cries of our fellow-men.
> Some would not stir from the ground, when they
> were lashed and beat in the most horrible man-
> ner.[300]

During the journey across the sea, Cugoano and others planned to burn down the ship but this plan was
discovered:

> When we found ourselves at last taken away, death
> was more preferable than life, and a plan was con-
> certed amongst us, that we might burn and blow

up the ship, and to perish all together in the flames; but we were betrayed by one of our own country-women, who slept with some of the head men of the ship, for it was common for the dirty filthy sailors to take the African women and lie upon their bodies; but the men were chained and pent up in holes.[301]

At Grenada, in America, where Cugoano was taken, he witnessed many acts of cruelty against Africans. The African slaves were often lashed and sometimes their teeth were knocked out if they were discovered eating sugar cane. Cugoano was lucky, though, because in less than two years he was brought to London and got his freedom from slavery about that time. He thanked God and the man who brought him to England, Alexander Campbell, for this, "Thanks be to God, I was delivered from Grenada, and that horrid brutal slavery – A gentleman coming to England, took me for his servant, and brought me away, where I soon found my situation become more agree-able." [302]

Now in England, Cugoano applied himself to learn-ing how to read and write:

> After coming to England, and seeing others write and read, I had a strong desire to learn, and getting what assistance I could, I applied myself to learn reading and writing, which soon became my recre-ation, pleasure, and delight; and when my master perceived that I could write some, he sent me to a proper school for that purpose to learn.[303]

After learning to read and write, Cugoano turned his mind towards the suffering of his fellow Africans. His book *Thoughts and Sentiments* was the first book written by an African criticising slavery and the slave trade. In many parts of the book, he points out facts that would not have been widely known by British people. He pointed out that merchants from Liverpool and Bristol were particularly barbaric. For them taking away the life of a black man was no more than taking away the life of a beast. And he gave the example of a trial in 1780 of a captain who ordered 132 Africans to be tied up in twos and thrown into the sea alive, so he could claim insurance:

> On the trial, by the counsel for the owners of the vessel against the underwriters, their argument was, that the slaves were to be considered the same as horses; and their plea for throwing them into the sea, was nothing better than that it might be more necessary to throw them overboard to lighten their vessel than goods of greater value or something to that effect.[304]

The slaves, Cugoano pointed out, were tied up in twos to ensure that they could not swim.

He pointed out that since the English took the lead in the slave trade, the number of slaves sold has massively increased. He writes:

> They have computed, that the ships from Liverpool, Bristol and London have exported from the coast of Africa upwards of one hundred thousand slaves annually; and that among other evils attending this

barbarous inhuman traffic, it is also computed that the numbers which are killed by the treacherous and barbarous methods of procuring them, together with those that perish in the voyage, and die in the seasoning, amount to at least an hundred thousand.[305]

Cugoano described how a British company called the Royal African Company which was set up by the British government and supported by the king had built many forts on the coast of Africa for keeping and trading slaves. The conditions in which the slaves were kept in these forts, Cugoano found too horrible to describe. He wondered how the French, the English, the Spaniards and the Portuguese could join hands to rob Africa of its sons and daughters.[306]

In the book, Cugoano set out his view that slavery was a grievous evil that needed to be stopped immediately. He pointed out that slavery denies Africans their natural rights as human beings. Hence, he implored the people of Britain:

> To take away that evil that your enemies, as well as our oppressors, are doing towards us, and cause them to desist from their evil treatment of the poor and despised Africans, before it be too late; and to restore that justice and liberty which is our natural rights.[307]

A point he made over and over in the book is that slavery is against the laws of God. For this reason, he often criticised Britain and its legislatures for protecting by law

something which is against the laws of God. He wondered
why a country which makes the stealing of men's property
illegal allows the stealing of men themselves to happen.
He believed every British person was guilty if they did
nothing about this cruel law:

> Where such a dreadful pre-eminence of iniquity
> abounds, as the admission of laws for tolerating
> slavery and wickedness, and the worst robberies, not
> only of men's properties, but themselves, and the
> many inhuman murders and cruelties occasioned
> by it; if it meets with your approbation, it is your
> sin…[308]

He wondered how a country which is widely considered to be civilised can be so barbaric in its dealing with
black people and warned that this "national wickedness"
will be met with a "national punishment" from God.

Somebody who knew Cugoano described him as a
godly, gentle, honest and very talented man. Among the
four Africans, he used Christian argument in his discussion most frequently. He pointed out in his book that
Britain and its church were not living up to the principles
of their Christian religion on this issue. There was no
point going to church frequently to pray if at the same
time you are oppressing defenceless people:

> Why think ye prayers in churches and chapels only
> will do ye good, if your charity do not extend to pity
> and regard your fellow creatures perishing through
> ignorance, under the heavy yoke of subjection and
> bondage.[309]

He was particularly critical of clergymen who would not speak out against what was happening. They would be guilty in the highest degree if they were found supporting slavery. But from his experience, most of the clergy were useless:

> I am sorry to find among Christians, and I think it is a great deficiency among the clergy in general, when covetous and profligate men are admitted amongst them, who either do not know, or dare not speak the truth, but neglect their duty much, or do it with such supineness, that it becomes good for nothing. Sometimes an old woman selling matches, will preach a better, and more orthodox sermon, than some of the clergy.[310]

Cugoano's book is a very comprehensive discussion of the argument against slavery; possibly the most comprehensive that exists. We can not describe all his views in this short volume. Among other things, he pointed out that abolition would be to the economic benefit of the British people, because they could form alliances with kingdoms in Africa and sell their goods to them and, also, free Africans would be more productive; he pointed out that slavery had a corrupting influence on the things that it touched, it had already corrupted some Africans and made them collaborators with white slave traders, and if not stopped, it would corrupt the British political system and constitution; he rejected that the fact that Africans kept slaves themselves was a good reason to enslave them, pointing out that Africans only keep people they capture during wars as slaves because they were forbidden to kill in cold blood, and they look after the people concerned very well.

One claim by supporters of slavery rebutted by Cugoano which is worth discussing further is that Africans were an ignorant people and by taking them into slavery they were helped to get knowledge and become more civilised than they would have been in Africa. Cugoano addressed this argument by first pointing out that even if Africans were ignorant it was no reason to hold them as slaves. You cannot dispel ignorance by treating people like animals, he argued.

> Some few, indeed, may eventually arrive at some knowledge of the Christian religion, and the great advantage of it. Such was the case of Ukawsaw Gronniosaw, an African prince, who lived in England. He was a long time in a state of great poverty and distress, and must have died at one time for want, if a good and charitable Attorney had not supported him. He was long after in a very poor state, but he would not have given his faith in the Christian religion, in exchange for all the kingdoms of Africa, if they could have been given to him, in place of his poverty.[311]

But such faith is due to the kindness of God, who gives grace to an African in spite of his enslavement. It should not be seen as a positive outcome of slavery. It has never been the intention of those who enslave African to make them better people:

It is not the intention of those who bring them away to make them better by it; nor is the design of slave-holders of any other intention, but that they may serve them as a kind of engines and beasts of burden.[312]

Cugoano, nonetheless, took the Christian education of fellow Africans in both Africa and Britain, seriously. He believed that true liberation of African people everywhere lay in them acquiring Christian education. In one edition of his book, *Thoughts and Sentiments*, Cugoano, referring to himself in the third person, describes his intention to open a school for the Christian education of fellow Africans in England:

He further proposed to open a school, for all such of his Complexion as are desirous of being acquainted with the Knowledge of the Christian Religion and the Laws of Civilisation. His sole Motive for these Undertakings, are, that he finds several of his Countrymen, here in England, who have not only been in an unlawful Manner brought away from their peaceable Habitations, but also deprived of every Blessing of the Christian Knowledge.[313]

This was a matter very close to his heart:

Nothing engages my desire so much as the Descendants of my Countrymen, so as to have them educated in the Duties and Knowledge of that Religion which all good Christian People enjoy…[314]

Regarding the school, he made this plea for financial support from his readers:

> I must wholly depend on the humane and charitable
> Contributions of those Ladies and Gentlemen who
> are inclinable to Support this Undertaking. I am
> not excluding some other young Persons, who need
> to be taught Reading, etc, but my Design is chiefly
> intended for my Countrymen.[315]

Regarding the Christian education of Africans in Africa, he suggested that well trained ministers be sent from Britain to Africa for that purpose. The people chosen for this purpose should not be people who are only well learned but people of good character:

> Their own learning, though the more the better, is
> not so much required as that they should be men of
> the same mind and principles of the apostle Paul;
> men that would hate covetousness, and who would
> hazard their lives for the cause and gospel of our
> Lord and Saviour Jesus Christ.[316]

It was also important to him that what is passed on to those being converted is scriptural, and not church traditions that have built up over the years in Europe:

> Teaching would be exceedingly necessary to the
> pagan nations and ignorant people in every place
> and situation; but they do not need any unscrip-
> tural forms and ceremonies to be taught them; they
> can devise superstitions [i.e. church traditions and

ceremonies] enough among themselves, and church
government too, if ever they need any.[317]

Apart from these things he did or tried to do on his
own, he worked closely with other people in the abolition
movement. He was a close friend of Equiano and a col-
league of his in the fight for abolition. He was a member
of the black group called the Sons of Africa who were agi-
tating for abolition and he co-signed many of their letters
to members of parliament and to white abolitionists. He
also worked with the white abolitionist Sharp and was
recorded in one of Sharp's biographies as having reported
to Sharp the case of a black man who had been kidnapped
and was going to be shipped to a Caribbean island.

In conclusion, Ottobah Cugoano saw slavery as a terrible evil which needed to be resisted robustly. An early
sign of his attitude showed aboard the slave ship taking
him and others to America, when he was among a group
that plotted to set it on fire. When he found himself freed
and living in relative comfort in England he used the
opportunity to acquire learning. He used that learning to
write his book *Thoughts and Sentiments* which was the first
public criticism of the slave trade by a black man and, possibly, the most comprehensive discussion of arguments on
slavery and the slave trade that exists. The benefits he got
from his own learning, perhaps, taught him that the true
liberation of African people everywhere lay in acquiring
education. For this reason he had the intention of opening a school specifically for educating African people in
England, and he made suggestions for the Christian education of other peoples around the world.

Closing Remarks

As we have done in previous chapters, we will now imagine the four Africans in a joint presentation about their attitude to slavery. Sancho, very much aware that this could be their most difficult joint presentation might begin with humour. He might point out that in the company of Equiano and Cugoano, it would be difficult for anybody to look good on this issue. Then he would say that it is important that people bear in mind his situation and the time in which he lived when considering his attitude and his contribution. For a start he was not born in Africa and so did not have any African memories to fall back on. Then, both his parents died when he was only two-years-old, meaning that he grew up and spent his life in English households. In spite of this, he saw slavery as wrong. He would point to his letter to Sterne, encouraging him to write more against slavery, as evidence of his view. He might also point to the help he gave to other Africans, like Soubise, who he helped to get a job as a butler, as proof that in spite of the impression he sometimes gave, he was happy to be African.

Gronniosaw would begin by pointing out that an important fact which Sancho had not mentioned was that they all lived at different times in Britain. He would say that if one considers that Sancho lived the prime of his life before the fight for abolition gathered pace, then it is worth bearing in mind that he, Gronniosaw, was already living in slavery as a teenager before Sancho was born. There were fewer black people around at the time to get support from, which was why he always trusted in God.

He would say that he, like the others, believed slavery was wrong, but he never had the safe space to express such a view. What he did was to make the most of his situation, by trying to be loyal to whoever was his master and to get on with the people around him.

Equiano would get up to speak, perhaps, to the sound of gentle applause. He would say that his own experience of being a slave and what he saw of how other Africans were being treated convinced him of how bad slavery was. This, he would say, was what he tried to convey in his book. He was sure people in far away Britain, who were reaping the benefits of the slave trade, did not fully know the atrocities that were being committed to give them those benefits. That revelation, he would suggest, was ultimately why the book was so successful. Its success lay not in his story or his writing, but in the fact that for the first time the life of a real slave was laid bare before the eyes of British people. To their credit, many British people took up the challenge to campaign for abolition. He would say that what he found most disturbing was the way slavery corrupted whatever it touched. Both Europeans and Africans were corrupted by the money from this trade. After all, he would remind them, the three people who came over the compound wall to kidnap him and his sisters were fellow Africans. This is not to diminish what Africa lost, he would say. He knew Africa lost a great deal of people and endured huge pain. He often wondered how his own mother felt the day she came home to discover he was gone.

He still, however, thinks the greatest damage slavery did was to human dignity. It lowered what it meant to be human. Slavery achieved this on both sides, because while the Africans were made to look less human by the degrading treatment they received, many Europeans were dehumanised by the level of wickedness the trade demanded of them. This, he would suggest, was probably why the abolition movement involved both black and white people. Many of them involved in that movement had perceived it as a threat to something dear and common, namely, their humanity. It is important therefore that this is not simply seen as a white versus black issue, but rather an issue of evil against good – the evil of slavery against the good of the shared sense of humanity. It is probably true today that black and white people still suffer from the memory of that awful time. Many black people would, justifiably, feel angry at what was done to their ancestors, while many Europeans would be ashamed at what was done by theirs.

Cugoano would begin by agreeing with Equiano's points. He would, however, add that such magnanimity should not mask what Africans and the African continent has endured through slavery, nor should it mask the fact that the intellectual supporters of slavery had to be engaged, robustly. It was, after all, Africans that were enslaved, and it was Africans that died in their millions. Africans may well have been involved in the industry but it was sponsored by European money, right up to the raids in African villages. He would point out that what could have prevented this and other great evils in history is people staying close to God. He was sure the British stooped so low because they had wandered off from God and no longer paid attention to God's laws. This was also relevant to Africans, he would say. This was why he had planned to open a school for their Christian education. Ultimately, Africa's protection against such atrocities as slavery lies in the hands of Africans, in staying close to God and getting themselves educated.

CHAPTER 7:
CONCLUDING
REMARKS

There is much more than can be understood from the writings of these four Africans than we can explore in this volume. What we will do at this point is to draw a few insights from their writings for today.

1 The value of identity

One issue which arises out of their stories is the issue of identity. From all accounts, it was a common practice among slave owners to destroy the sense of identity of the Africans they had bought to use as slaves as a way of breaking them. Key to this was to change the name of the slave. They were also forced to abandon their African language and cultural practices. This was the master's way of saying that the slave's life before that moment has been blotted out and a new life was beginning at that moment. It is interesting to observe that three of the four

Africans when they got their freedom reverted to their African names (Sancho, for no fault of his, never had an African name), in order to get back what they had lost. This is relevant to the debate in Britain and other countries today about how to integrate people from different ethnic groups. There is probably a natural process whereby people gradually give up aspects of the culture they brought with them to adopt aspects of the culture of where they are. What has to be avoided is any sense that people were being "forced" to jettison the culture of their origin and adopt the host culture wholesale in order to make progress. That would deprive them of the sense of identity they get from their first culture and could be too heavy a price to pay to make progress in life.

2 Racism

A point the slaves made repeatedly was that they too were human beings. This point would sound strange to many people today, but during the slavery era it was very important. At the time they wrote their books, many European scientists were going around saying that black people did not belong to the human species. They placed black people midway between apes and human beings, sometimes nearer apes than human beings. The Swedish botanist Carl Linne, who laid the basis for the modern classification of plants and animals, arranged human beings in a hierarchy that was largely based on skin colour, with white people at the top.[318] Other scientists used other physical characteristics, but always making sure that the physical characteristics they chose was one that gave them the result they wanted. This is, in fact, the original meaning of "racism", that is, the separation of people into different species or "races" based on their skin colour or other characteristics. The "racists" held the view that people with black skin were of a sub-human species, between the human race and the animal race.

That classification was important because it would enable white people to maltreat black people without having to deal with feelings arising out of their common humanity. Experience shows that there is something about our common humanity (perhaps a kind of "family bond") which makes it difficult for human beings to maltreat each other. The sense of common humanity is a barrier when a human being wants to oppress another. This is probably why when people want to oppress others, they begin by de-humanising them, that is, convincing themselves that the people they want to oppress were not human like them. Countries who want to go to war, often prepare by de-humanising their enemies. This tends to have the effect of breaking the bond of a common humanity and freeing the country up to attack their enemies, mercilessly.

3 Modern Slavery

The point was made by the Africans that before their life stories as slaves were published, British people who got the benefit of the trade went about their life in ignorance. This is a point relevant to our modern life today. Increasingly, goods are produced in one part of the world and transported for use in another. If people only think about how cheaply they buy these goods from the market, and give no consideration to the possible conditions of the workers producing them, they may end up making the same mistake of the British public of the slavery era. In fact, anti-slavery organisations continue to reveal that there are forms of slavery that are still going on today. The campaign group Anti Slavery International has pointed out that in 2007, over 12 million people were living and working under contemporary forms of slavery, as defined by international law. That means that the issue of slavery is not just in the past. Each person today could still find out what they could do or what the government that represents them could do to stop modern slavery.

4 Religion and Social Action

Another point the slaves made is how our religious beliefs affect our behaviour. They pointed out repeatedly that religion that does not translate into treating people humanely was worthless. Cugoano criticised religious ministers who, instead of speaking up for oppressed people were more interested in the trappings of their office. Christianity and other religions have a view of God as a being that is just and fair. That means that anybody who stands aside to watch people being oppressed is not really serving their God. Sadly, far from defending the oppressed, the most religious people are sometimes the most oppressive. In this case, religion can be used to relieve the feeling of guilt and make people more able to oppress. A good symbol of this kind of religion is Elmina castle, in Ghana. Elmina was one of over twenty forts in the shoreline of Ghana, where Africans were held as slaves before being shipped to America. Standing in the middle of the castle, surrounded by slave dungeons, was a church. At this church, the slave traders worshipped God regularly. One can only hope that Christians today and practitioners of other religions put their religion to better use than the slave traders at Elmina.

Postscript:
Equiano's Nigerian Origin Discovered?

An issue that is yet unresolved regarding Equiano is where in Nigeria he was born. Two hundred years ago, when he wrote his book, the name Nigeria and many other common names we have today did not exist. Much of West Africa, from where slaves were taken, was called Guinea. It is also common to locate areas within this large sway of land by reference to the powerful kingdoms in the region. This is what Equiano did. In his book, Equiano describe his place of origin in these words:

> The part of Africa, known by the name Guinea, to which the trade for slaves is carried on, extends along the coast above 3400 miles, from Senegal to Angola, and includes a variety of kingdoms. Of these the most considerable is the kingdom of Benin, both as to extent and wealth, the richness and cultivation of the soil, the power of its king, and the number and warlike disposition of the inhabit-

ants... This kingdom is divided into many provinces or districts: in one of the most remote and fertile of which, called Eboe, I was born, in the year 1745, in a charming fruitful vale, named Essaka. The distance of the province from the capital of Benin and the sea coast must be very considerable; for I had never heard of white men or Europeans, nor of the sea: and our subjection to the king of Benin was little more than nominal.[319]

From this we learn that 1) the influence of the kingdom of Benin reached his place of origin, 2) the land itself was called Eboe, and 3) his village was called Essaka.

Regarding the first point, we know that present day Benin, which was the centre of the Benin kingdom, is in southern Nigeria. On the second point, his land of origin which he referred to as Eboe is widely believed by scholars to be the Ibo (pronounced Igbo) land of south-eastern Nigeria. (See Map 1 for Benin and Igbo land.) The view that Equiano came from the Igbo land is supported by the fact that both his names "Olaudah" and "Equiano" are Igbo names, even though aspects of the spelling might have been Anglicised; the African names that he gave to people and events in his description of his childhood are recognisable Igbo names and, the customs he described of village life have been recognised as Igbo customs.

What has been difficult is locating where exactly he came from within the Igbo (or Ibo) land. The first issue is whether he came from the Igbo area west of the River Niger (called Ika Igbo) or east of the River Niger. (See Map 1.) Regarding this, James Walvin writes:

Equiano is thought to be an Ibo from the northern Ika Ibo district, in what today is the eastern province of Benin, Nigeria. Tropical rain country, the area was criss-crossed by trade routes, one of them leading south by foot, thence by the River Ase and on to the major slave-trading region of the coast.[320]

Walvin's view is that Equiano is from an area west of the Niger River, hence west of the city of Ontisha which is at the eastern bank of the River. See Map 2. That would be suggested by Equiano's reference to the influence of Benin kingdom. However, the Benin kingdom was a powerful kingdom at the time reaching far and wide. Equiano, himself, reminds us that it was the "most considerable" in the whole of West Africa. As the "nominal" influence of the kingdom of Benin reached into Onitsha and farther east, Equiano's reference to Benin should not be seen as excluding areas east of Onitsha.

The view that Equiano came from an area east of Onitsha is, in fact, what has received more support among scholars of the subject. That was the view expressed by Paul Edwards in his Introduction to *The Life of Olaudah Equiano*. Edwards, who has collaborated with Walvin in the past, and who on his own republished Equiano's story, twice, has studied this subject extensively. It is, in fact, Edward's own publication of Equiano's story, *The Life of Olaudah Equiano,* that other researchers have often used as their source. Edwards also makes up his understanding of Igbo culture and names by drawing on the knowledge of a number of Igbo contacts, including Chinua Achebe, the renowned novelist, who is an Igbo man. From his research, Edwards suggests that Equiano came from somewhere east of Onitsha and this is where his village, Essaka, would be found.

One of Edwards's pieces of evidence is based on this description by Equiano of a coin which his people use for trading:

> In such state money is of little use; however we have some small pieces of coin, if I may call them such. They are made something like an anchor; but I do not remember either their value or denomination.[321]

Drawing on other works about the area, Edwards writes:

> A feature of the description Equiano could not have found in contemporary accounts is the coinage 'something like an anchor' which suggests the location of Essaka as somewhere to the east of Onitsha, a view shared by Achebe: the coinage would appear to be the 'umumu currency consisting of tiny arrow shaped pieces of iron' noted by Forde and Jones as still found in the eastern Onitsha region; they are also mentioned by Basden as being found 'between Awka and Enugu'.[322]

An attempt to locate Equiano's Essaka village more precisely has been made by Catherine Acholonu. Acholonu, who is Igbo, has suggested that Equiano's village is, in fact, a place called Isseke. She argued that the same way Equiano misspelled "Ibo" (or "Igbo") as "Eboe" he has probably misspelled "Isseke" as "Essaka". Acholonu also found a family called Ekwealua who she believed to be the family Equiano came from. These two findings, that is, the Isseke village and the Ekwealua family convinced Acholonu that she has found Equiano's origin. Hence she writes:

> As I delved deeper and deeper into the two-hundred-dred-year-old secret which Isseke had harbored unnoticed, I realised that there was no point in searching further. Here on the primeval soil of this special ancient people of Isseke, Olaude Ekwealuo had been born some two hundred and fifty years ago.[323]

The two names, Equiano and Ekwealuo, are more similar than they may appear to non-Igbo eyes. The Igbo language does not have the letter "q" in its alphabets. The "q" sound is produced with "kw". Also the letters "n" and "l" are used interchangeably in Igbo language. Although Acholonu's view that the village named by Equiano as "Essaka" is the present day "Isseke" has a technical weakness[324], we should still remain open to the possibility that her findings are right.

Edwards, however, holds a different view about Equiano's village. Regarding the name "Essaka", Edwards writes:

> I suspect that the name of Equiano's home village is a derivative of Awka. Place names such as Ezi-Awka, still to be found in the area, might well have been Anglicised into Essaka.[325]

Following Edwards's line of thought, I have found such a village. It is called Ezioka (pronounced Ezi-Awka). It is in a town called Isu Awaa which is not only east of Onitsha, but lies between Awka and Enugu – the area the *umumu* currency referred to by Equiano has been found. Isu Awaa is in what used to be Awgu Local Government Area of Enugu State, Nigeria. Due to recent boundary changes it is now in Mbanabo Local Government Area. It is surrounded by the following town: Ituku, Agbogwugwu, Ihe and Agbudu. What is interesting about the name of the village (i.e. Ezi Awka) is that the way Equiano has written it, "Essaka", is exactly the way the villagers pronounce it, and so the way it would have been called in Equiano's days. If this is Equiano's place of origin, it would mean that he had not Anglicised the name as Edwards has suggested, rather he has written it out the way it is pronounced – much like writing the Igbo names "Ijeoma" and "Ifeoma" as "Ijoma" and "Ifoma" or the names of the English cities "Leicester" and "Gloucester" as "Lester" and "Gloster".

A reference to "Ezioka" can be found in a recent book by a member of that village, a man called Harford Ugwu. This is what he wrote on page 68 of his book, *Change is Possible*:

> I was born into a pagan family, one of the three that serve as high priest to the Town's Shrine, in order of seniority. 'Umu Chineke' the children of God in Ezioka village whose role in Isu Awaa represents those of the Levites of old...[326]

I have attached an image of that page.

Two other important facts are that I have met a man in that village whose name is Ekwuno (pronounced Equno). This man is alive and currently in his forties. This is not to suggest that Olaudah Equiano, if he came from this very village, is related to this man. It is only to point out that the name, which is not widely used among Igbo people, exists within this village. In any case, Equno (or Ekwuno) is only this man's first name and might not have any historical significance for his lineage. Secondly, the villagers tell a story of two siblings who were "sold" into slavery long ago. Because there are no written records, this is, however, too far in the past for the details to be remembered.

In conclusion, here we have 1) a village with exactly the name suggested by Edwards and 2) at the general location he has suggested, 3) evidence that the name exists in the village and 4) a story of two siblings lost to slavery and never seen again. In a society where written record is relatively new, we might never know for sure where Equiano came from. However, these four facts make this case sufficiently significant for me to place it in the public domain.

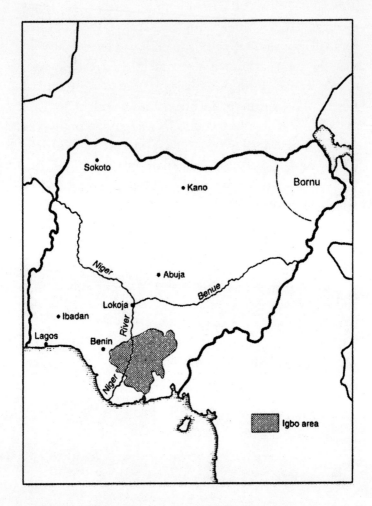

Map 1. Nigeria, showing the Igbo area

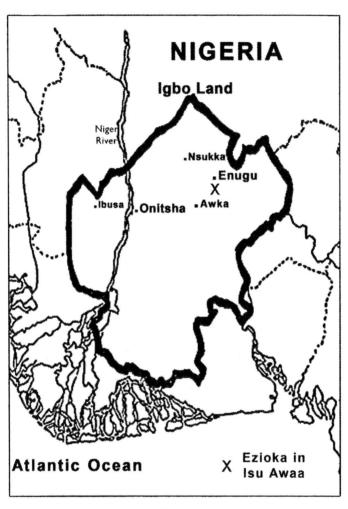

Map 2

Map 2

Chapter Six

MY TESTIMONY

I was born into a pagan family, one of the three that serve as high priest to the Town's Shrine, in order of seniority. "Umu Chineke" the children of God in Ezioka village whose role in Isu Awaa represents those of the Levites of old but they turned away from the way of truth. This misleading role was all I grew up to learn, and was made to believe. Christianity was a mere formality. The whole town believed, trusted and had faith in their traditional religion.

Being a Christian, especially belonging to EFAC or SU was a matter of very serious offence in the 80's. All the youths in my village were prohibited from belonging to any such groups, and parents were warned to monitor their children.

Almost all priests posted to the town suffered ejection for not respecting the traditions of the land. Preaching against idol worship was the offence. Under this background, the three families in my village, guarded this heritage with their heart and soul.

Anyone who violated the laws was ostracized. Some issues were blown up into police and court cases, that lasted for very many years, financed by the village.

I was a pioneer and executive member of my village

BIBLIOGRAPHY

Acholonu, C O *The Igbo Roots of Olaudah Equiano* Owerri, Nigeria: Afa, 1989.

Anstey, R *The Atlantic Slave Trade and British Abolition 1760-1810* London, Macmillan Press, 1975.

Cugoano, Ottobah *Thoughts and Sentiments on the Evil and Wicked Traffic of the Slavery and Commerce of the Human Species Humbly Submitted to the Inhabitants of Great Britain* London, 1787.

Cugoano, Ottobah *Thoughts and Sentiments on the Evil and Wicked Traffic of the Slaver* edited with Introduction by Paul Edwards, London: Dawsons of Pall Mall, 1969.

Cugoano, Ottobah *Thoughts and Sentiments on the Evil and Wicked Traffic of the Slavery and Commerce of the Human Species*, with Introduction and Notes by Vincent Carreta, 1999.

Equiano, Olaudah *The Interesting Narrative of the Life of Olaudah Equiano or Gustavus Vassa The African* London 1789 (in two volumes).

Equiano, Olaudah *The Interesting Narrative and other Writings by Olaudah Equiano* edited with Introduction by Vincent Carreta, London: Penguin, 1995.

Equiano Olaudah *The Life of Olaudah Equiano* (ed) Paul Edward Harlow, England: Pearson Educational Limited, 1988.

Fryer, P *Staying Power* London Pluto Press, 1984.

Gronniosaw, Ukawsaw *Narrative of the Most Remarkable particulars in the Life of James Albert Ukawsaw Gronniosaw an African Prince as Related by Himself.* Leeds, 1811.

Lartey, S "Elmina Castle" in Ontario Black History Society website (www.blackhistorysociety.ca).

Sancho, Ignatius *Letters of the Late Ignatius Sancho An African* (in two volumes0 London 1782.

Sancho, Ignatius *The Letters of Ignatius Sancho* edited with Introduction by Paul Edwards and Polly Rewt, Edinburgh: Edinburgh University Press, 1994.

Ugwu, H *Change is Possible* Hax: Enugu, Nigeria, 2004.

Walvin, J *Black Ivory* Oxford: Blackwell Publishers, 2001.

Notes

Chapter 1:
Introduction

[1] Fryer, *Staying Power,* p15.

[2] Anstey, *The Atlantic Slave Trade and the British Abolition in 1760-1810*, pxix.

[3] Lartey, S Ontario Black History Society (www.blackhistorysociety.ca).

[4] Walvin, *Black Ivory*, p81.

[5] Walvin, *Black Ivory*, p81.

[6] Anstey R, *The Atlantic Slave Trade and the British Abolition in 1760-1810*, pxix.

[7] Black Ivory, p276.

[8] Sancho, *Letters of the Late Ignatius Sancho*, p60.

[9] Sancho, *Letters of the Late Ignatius Sancho*, p61.

[10] Gronniosaw, *The Life of Gronniosaw,* p27.

[11] Equiano, *Interesting Narrative*, vol 1, p206.

[12] Cugoano, *Thoughts and Sentiments*, p30.

Chapter 2:
Meet the Characters

[13] Jekyll's *Life of Ignatius Sancho*. in *Letters of the Late Ignatius Sancho*, vol 1, pvi.

[14] *Letters of the Late Ignatius Sancho*, vol 1, pvi.

[15] *Letters of the Late Ignatius Sancho*, vol 1, pvi.

[16] *Letters of the Late Ignatius Sancho*, vol 1, pvi.

[17] Fryer, *Staying Power*, p93. The first book in English language by a black writer was Briton Hammon's *Narrative of the Uncommon Sufferings and Surprising Deliverance of Briton Hammon,* but this was published in Boston, USA.

[18] Sancho in Edwards and Rewt ed., p45.

[19] Sancho, *Letters of the Late Ignatius Sancho*, vol 2, p1.

[20] Sancho, *Letters of the Late Ignatius Sancho*, vol 2, p4.

[21] Edwards and Rewt's "Introduction" to Edwards and Rewt (ed.) *The Letters of Ignatius Sancho*, p3-4.

[22] Fryer, *Staying Power,* p89.

[23] Fryer, *Staying Power,* p 89.

[24] Gronniosaw, *The Life of Gronniosaw*, p7.

[25] Gronniosaw, *The Life of Gronniosaw,* p10.

[26] Fryer, *Staying Power*, p89.

[27] Fryer, *Staying Power*, p90.

[28] "Preface" to *The Life of Gronniosaw*, p4.

[29] Fryer, *Staying Power*, p102.

[30] Equiano, *Interesting Narrative*, vol 1, p48.

[31] Fryer, *Staying Power,* p103.

[32] Fryer, *Staying Power,* p104.

[33] Fryer, *Staying Power,* p106.

[34] Fryer, *Staying Power,* p106.

[35] Fryer, *Staying Power,* p106.

[36] Fryer, *Staying Power,* p108.

[37] Fryer: *Staying Power,* p108.

[38] Fryer, *Staying Power,* p107.

[39] Fryer, *Staying Power,* p111.

[40] Fryer, *Staying Power,* p98.

[41] Edwards (ed.) *Thoughts and Sentiments*: pv.

[42] Edwards (ed.) *Thoughts and Sentiments*, pvii.

[43] Fryer, *Staying Power,* p98.

[44] Fryer, *Staying Power,* p100.

[45] Cugoano, *Thoughts and Sentiments*, p75-76.

[46] Fryer, *Staying Power*, p100.

[47] Edwards's "Introduction" to Edwards (ed.) *Thoughts and Sentiments*, viii.

[48] Fryer, *Staying Power,* p101.

[49] Fryer, *Staying Power,* p99.

[50] Cugoano, *Thoughts and Sentiments*, p21.

Chapter 3:
Attitude to Christianity

[51] Sancho, *Letters of the Late Ignatius Sancho*, p114.

[52] Sancho, *Letters of the Late Ignatius Sancho*, p114.

[53] Sancho, *Letters of the Late Ignatius Sancho*, p114-115.

[54] Sancho, *Letters of the Late Ignatius Sancho*, p82.

[55] Sancho, *Letters of the Late Ignatius Sancho*, p181.

56 Sancho, *Letters of the Late Ignatius Sancho*, vol 1, p124

57 Sancho, *Letters of the Late Ignatius Sancho*, vol 1, p126.

58 Sancho, *Letters of the Late Ignatius Sancho*, vol 2, p38.

59 Sancho, *Letters of the Late Ignatius Sancho*, pvol2, p2.

60 Sancho, *Letters of the Late Ignatius Sancho*, vol 2, p147.

61 Sancho, *Letters of the Late Ignatius Sancho*, vol 1, p4.

62 Sancho, *Letters of the Late Ignatius Sancho*, vol 2, p114.

63 Sancho, *Letters of Ignatius Sancho*, vol 1, p155.

64 Sancho, *Letters of the Late Ignatius Sancho*, vol 1, p156.

65 Sancho, *Letters of the Late Ignatius Sancho*, vol 1, p47.

66 Sancho, *Letters of the Late Ignatius Sancho*, vol 1, p80.

67 Sancho, *Letters of the Late Ignatius Sancho*, vol 1, p56.

68 Sancho, *Letters of the Late Ignatius Sancho*, vol 1, p108.

69 From Edwards and Rewt (ed.) *The Letters of Ignatius Sancho*, p158.

70 Sancho, *Letters of the Late Ignatius Sancho*, vol 1, p43-44.

71 Sancho, *Letters of the Late Ignatius Sancho*, vol 1, p37-38.

72 Sancho, *The Letters of the Late Ignatius Sancho*, vol 1, p150.

73 Sancho, *Letters of the Late Ignatius Sancho*, vol 1, p50.

74 Sancho, *Letters of the Late Ignatius Sancho*, vol 1, p69.

75 Sancho, *Letters of the Late Ignatius Sancho*, vol 1, p980.

76 Gronniosaw, *The Life of Gronniosaw*, p4.

77 Gronniosaw, *The Life of Gronniosaw*, p5.

78 Gronniosaw, *The Life of Gronniosaw*, p16.

79 Gronniosaw, *The Life of Gronniosaw*, p16.

80 Gronniosaw, *The Life of Gronniosaw*, p16.

81 Gronniosaw, *The Life of Gronniosaw*, p4.

[82] Gronniosaw, *The Life of Gronniosaw,* p11.

[83] Gronniosaw, *The Life of Gronniosaw,* p12.

[84] The words of John the Baptist in John 1:29.

[85] Gronniosaw, *The Life of Gronniosaw,* p16.

[86] Gronniosaw, *The Life of Gronniosaw,* p18. A reference to Col 2:10.

[87] Gronniosaw, *The Life of Gronniosaw,* p18.

[88] Gronniosaw, *The Life of Gronniosaw,* p10.

[89] Gronniosaw, *The Life of Gronniosaw,* p28.

[90] Gronniosaw, *The Life of Gronniosaw,* p29.

[91] Equiano, *Interesting Narrative*, vol 1, p133.

[92] *A Guide to the Indians*, written by Bishop Thomas Wilson, London 1740.

[93] Equiano, *Interesting Narrative*, vol 1, p240.

[94] Equiano, *Interesting Narrative*, vol 1, p 86.

[95] Versions of the Golden Rule can also be found in other religions, however, they tend to be stated in the negative, that is, "Don't do to others what you would not like them to do to you". Jesus stated his version positively, that is, "Do to others…"

[96] Equiano, *Interesting Narrative*, vol 1, p215.

[97] Equiano, *Interesting Narrative*, vol 1, p222.

[98] Equiano, *Interesting Narrative*, vol 1, p93.

[99] Equiano, *Interesting Narrative*, vol 1, p259-260.

[100] Equiano, *Interesting Narrative*, vol 1, p235.

[101] Equiano, *Interesting Narrative*, vol 1, p 87.

[102] Equiano, *Interesting Narrative*, vol 1, p211-212.

[103] Equiano in Carreta (ed.) *The Interesting Narrative and other Writings*, p331.

[104] Equiano in Carreta (ed.) *The Interesting Narrative and other Writings*, p335.

[105] Equiano, *Interesting Narrative*, vol 1, p217-218.

[106] Equiano, *Interesting Narrative*, vol 1, p218.

[107] Equiano, *Interesting Narrative*, vol 1, p242.

[108] Equiano, *Interesting Narrative*, vol 1, p181.

[109] Cugoano, *Thoughts and Sentiments*, piv.

[110] Cugoano, *Thoughts and Sentiments*, p120.

[111] Cugoano, *Thoughts and Sentiments*, p105.

[112] Cugoano, *Thoughts and Sentiments*, p127.

[113] Cugoano, *Thoughts and Sentiments*, p63.

[114] Cugoano, *Thoughts and Sentiments*, p53.

[115] Cugoano, *Thoughts and Sentiments*, p30.

[116] Cugoano, *Thoughts and Sentiments*, p30.

[117] Cugoano, *Thoughts and Sentiments*, p30.

[118] Cugoano, *Thoughts and Sentiments*, p130.

[119] Cugoano, *Thoughts and Sentiments*, plv.

[120] Cugoano, *Thoughts and Sentiments*, 1791 Edition.

[121] Cugoano, *Thoughts and Sentiments*, p60.

[122] Cugoano, *Thoughts and Sentiments*, p60.

[123] Cugoano, *Thoughts and Sentiments*, p60.

[124] Cugoano, *Thoughts and Sentiments*, p114.

[125] Cugoano, *Thoughts and Sentiments*, p24.

[126] Cugoano, *Thoughts and Sentiments*, p24.

[127] Cugoano, *Thoughts and Sentiments*, p125.

[128] Cugoano, *Thoughts and Sentiments*, p95-96.

[129] Sancho in Edwards and Rewt (ed.) *The Letters of Ignatius Sancho*, p78.

Chapter 4:
Understanding of God

[130] Sancho, *Letters of the Late Ignatius Sancho*, vol 1, p95-96.

[131] Sancho, *Letters of the Late Ignatius Sancho*, vol 1, p186.

[132] Sancho, *Letters of the Late Ignatius Sancho*, vol 1, p184.

[133] Sancho, *Letters of the Late Ignatius Sancho*, vol 1, p82.

[134] Sancho, *Letters of the Late Ignatius Sancho*, vol 1, p48.

[135] Sancho, *Letters of the Late Ignatius Sancho*, vol 1, p100.

[136] Sancho, *Letters of the Late Ignatius Sancho*, vol 1, p186.

[137] Sancho, *Letters of the Late Ignatius Sancho*, vol 1, p78.

[138] Sancho, *Letters of the Late Ignatius Sancho*, vol 1, p119.

[139] Sancho, *Letters of the Late Ignatius Sancho*, vol 1, p117-118.

[140] Sancho, *Letters of the Late Ignatius Sancho*, vol 1, p102.

[141] Sancho, *Letters of the Late Ignatius Sancho*, vol 2, p27.

[142] Sancho, *Letters of the Late Ignatius Sancho*, vol 1, p45.

[143] Sancho, *Letters of the Late Ignatius Sancho*, vol 1, p33.

[144] Sancho, *Letters of the Late Ignatius Sancho*, vol 1, p37-38.

[145] Sancho, *Letters of the Late Ignatius Sancho*, vol 1, p4.

[146] Sancho, *Letters of the Late Ignatius Sancho*, Vol 2, p42.

[147] Sancho, *Letters of the Late Ignatius Sancho*, vol 1, p7.

[148] Sancho, *Letters of the Late Ignatius Sancho*, Vol 2, p2.

[149] Gronniosaw, *The Life of Gronniosaw,* p10.

[150] Gronniosaw, *The Life of Gronniosaw*, p29.

[151] Gronniosaw, *The Life of Gronniosaw*, p29.

[152] Gronniosaw, *The Life of Gronniosaw*, p10.

[153] Gronniosaw, *The Life of Gronniosaw*, p12.

[154] Gronniosaw, *The Life of Gronniosaw*, p27.

[155] Gronniosaw, *The Life of Gronniosaw*, p30

[156] Gronniosaw, *The Life of Gronniosaw*, p30.

[157] Gronniosaw, *The Life of Gronniosaw*, p18 A Reference to Col 2:10

[158] Gronniosaw, *The Life of Gronniosaw*, p17.

[159] Gronniosaw, *The Life of Gronniosaw*, p19.

[160] Gronniosaw, *The Life of Gronniosaw*, p20.

[161] Gronniosaw, *The Life of Gronniosaw*, p19.

[162] Gronniosaw, *The Life of Gronniosaw*, p22.

[163] Equiano, *Interesting Narrative*, vol 1, p159-160.

[164] Equiano, *Interesting Narrative*, vol 1, p116.

[165] Equiano, *Interesting Narrative*, vol 1, p264-265.

[166] Equiano, *Interesting Narrative*, vol 1, p265.

[167] Equiano, *Interesting Narrative*, vol 1, p117.

[168] Equiano, *Interesting Narrative*, vol 1, p216.

[168] Equiano, *Interesting Narrative*, vol 1, p181.

[169] Equiano in Carreta (ed.) *The Interesting Narrative and other Writings*: 328.

[170] Equiano in Carreta (ed.) *Interesting Narratives*: 332.

[171] Equiano in Carreta (ed.) *The Interesting narrative and other Writings*, (London: Penguin, 1995), p332.

[172] Equiano in Carreta (ed.) *The Interesting narrative and other Writings*, 329.

[173] Equiano, *Interesting Narrative*, vol 1, p181.

[174] Equiano, *Interesting Narrative*, vol 1, p242.

[175] Equiano, *Interesting Narrative*, vol 1, 243.

[176] Equiano, *Interesting Narrative*, vol 2, p254.

[177] Cugoano, *Thoughts and Sentiments*, p44.

[178] Cugoano, *Thoughts and Sentiments*, p128.

[179] Cugoano, *Thoughts and Sentiments*, p145.

[180] Cugoano, *Thoughts and Sentiments*, p129.

[181] Cugoano, *Thoughts and Sentiments*, p98.

[182] Cugoano, *Thoughts and Sentiments*, p4.

[183] Cugoano, *Thoughts and Sentiments*, p62-63.

[184] Cugoano, *Thoughts and Sentiments*, p64-65.

[185] Cugoano, *Thoughts and Sentiments*, p77.

[186] Cugoano, *Thoughts and Sentiments*, p44.

[187] Cugoano, *Thoughts and Sentiments*, p145.

[188] Cugoano, *Thoughts and Sentiments*, p110.

[189] Cugoano, *Thoughts and Sentiments*, p4.

[190] Cugoano, *Thoughts and Sentiments*, p110.

Chapter 5:
Understanding of Humanity

[191] Edwards and Rewt (ed.) *The Letters of Ignatius Sancho,* p158-159.

[192] Sancho, *Letters of the Late Ignatius Sancho*, vol 2, p62.

[193] From Edwards and Rewt (ed.) *The Letters of Ignatius Sancho*: 4.

[194] Sancho, *Letters of the Late Ignatius Sancho*, vol 2, p1.

[195] Sancho, *Letters of the Late Ignatius Sancho*, vol 1, p60.

[196] Sancho, *Letters of the Late Ignatius Sancho*, vol 1, p145.

[197] Sancho, *Letters of the Late Ignatius Sancho*, vol 2, p48.

[198] Sancho, *Letters of the Late Ignatius Sancho*, vol 1, p8.

[199] Sancho, *Letters of the Late Ignatius Sancho*, vol 1, p124.

[200] Sancho, *Letters of the Late Ignatius Sancho*, vol 1, p122.

[201] See notes from Edwards and Rewt (ed.) *The Letters of Ignatius Sancho*, p159.

[202] Turban or lawn sleeves, probably means "Asian or European".

[203] Sancho, *Letters of the Late Ignatius Sancho*, vol 1, p175.

[204] From Edwards and Rewt (ed.) *The Letters of Ignatius Sancho*, p138.

[205] Sancho, *Letters of the Late Ignatius Sancho*, vol 2, p5.

[206] Gronniosaw, *The Life of Gronniosaw*, p21-22.

[207] Gronniosaw, *The Life of Gronniosaw*, p22.

[208] Gronniosaw, *The Life of Gronniosaw*, p14.

[209] Gronniosaw, *The Life of Gronniosaw*, p15.

[210] Gronniosaw, *The Life of Gronniosaw*, p15.

[211] Gronniosaw, *The Life of Gronniosaw*, p15-16.

[212] Gronniosaw, *The Life of Gronniosaw*, p16.

[213] Gronniosaw, *The Life of Gronniosaw*, p18.

[214] Gronniosaw, *The Life of Gronniosaw*, p15.

[215] Gronniosaw, *The Life of Gronniosaw*, p4.

[216] Gronniosaw, *The Life of Gronniosaw*, p21.

[217] Gronniosaw, *The Life of Gronniosaw*, p21.

[218] Gronniosaw, *The Life of Gronniosaw*, p21.

[219] Gronniosaw, *The Life of Gronniosaw,* p25.

[220] Gronniosaw, *The Life of Gronniosaw,* p22.

[221] Gronniosaw, *The Life of Gronniosaw,* p22.

[222] Equiano, *Interesting Narrative*, vol 1, p2-3.

[223] Equiano, *Interesting Narrative*, vol 1, p5.

[224] Equiano, *Interesting Narrative*, vol 1, p32.

[225] Equiano, *Interesting Narrative*, vol 1, p213.

[226] Equiano, *Interesting Narrative*, vol 1, p220-221.

[227] Equiano, *Interesting Narrative.* vol 2, p66 -67.

[228] Equiano, *Interesting Narrative*, vol 2, p69-70.

[229] Equiano, *Interesting Narrative*,vol 2, p74.

[230] Equiano, *Interesting Narrative*, vol 2, p75-76.

[231] Equiano, *Interesting Narrative*, vol 1, p225.

[232] Equiano, *Interesting Narrative*, vol 1, p87-88.

[233] Cugoano, *Thoughts and Sentiments*, p60.

[234] Cugoano, *Thoughts and Sentiments*, p61.

[235] Cugoano, *Thoughts and Sentiments*, p61.

[236] Cugoano, *Thoughts and Sentiments*, p31.

[237] Cugoano, *Thoughts and Sentiments*, p32.

[238] Cugoano, *Thoughts and Sentiments*, p119.

[239] Cugoano, *Thoughts and Sentiments*, p32.

[240] Cugoano, *Thoughts and Sentiments*, p38.

[241] Cugoano, *Thoughts and Sentiments*, p29.

[242] Cugoano, *Thoughts and Sentiments*, p29.

[243] Cugoano, *Thoughts and Sentiments*, p62.

[244] Cugoano, *Thoughts and Sentiments*, p63.

[245] Cugoano, *Thoughts and Sentiments*, p21-22.

[246] Cugoano, *Thoughts and Sentiments*, p120.

[247] Cugoano, *Thoughts and Sentiments*, p120.

[248] Cugoano, *Thoughts and Sentiments*, p120.

[249] Cugoano, *Thoughts and Sentiments*, p5.

Chapter 6:
Attitude to Slavery

[250] Jekyll's *Life of Ignatius Sancho* printed in *Letters of the Late Ignatius Sancho*, vol 1, p22 .

[251] *Letters of the Late Ignatius Sancho*, vol 1, p22f.

[252] Sancho, *Letters of the Late Ignatius Sancho*, vol 1, p174.

[253] Sancho, *Letters of the Late Ignatius Sancho*, vol 1, p174.

[254] Sancho, *Letters of the Late Ignatius Sancho*, vol 1, p175.

[255] Sancho, *Letters of the Late Ignatius Sancho*, vol 1, p175.

[256] Fryer, *Staying Power*, p91.

[257] Fryer, *Staying Power*, p91.

[258] "Lionzed" i.e. treated as a celebrity.

[259] Fryer, *Staying Power*, p92.

[260] Fryer, *Staying Power*, p93.

[261] Sancho, *Letters of the Late Ignatius Sancho*, vol 1, p175-176.

[262] Sancho, *Letters of the Late Ignatius Sancho*, vol 1, p176.

[263] Sancho, *Letters of the Late Ignatius Sancho*, vol 1, p96-97.

[264] Sancho, *Letters of the Late Ignatius Sancho*, vol 1, p97.

[265] Sancho, *Letters of the Late Ignatius Sancho*, vol 1, p97.

266 Sancho, *Letters of the Late Ignatius Sancho*, vol 2, p169-170.

267 Sancho, *Letters of the Late Ignatius Sancho*, vol 1, p70.

268 Sancho, *Letters of the Late Ignatius Sancho*, vol 2, p3.

269 Gronniosaw, *The Life of Gronniosaw,* p11.

270 Gronniosaw, *The Life of Gronniosaw,* p11.

271 Gronniosaw, *The Life of Gronniosaw,* p11.

272 Gronniosaw, *The Life of Gronniosaw,* p12.

273 Gronniosaw, *The Life of Gronniosaw,* p13.

274 Gronniosaw, *The Life of Gronniosaw,* p17.

275 Gronniosaw, *The Life of Gronniosaw,* p24.

276 Gronniosaw, *The Life of Gronniosaw,* p11.

277 Gronniosaw, *The Life of Gronniosaw,* p13.

278 Gronniosaw, *The Life of Gronniosaw,* p12.

279 Gronniosaw, *The Life of Gronniosaw,* p12.

280 Equiano, *Interesting Narrative*, vol 1, p48.

281 Equiano, *Interesting Narrative*, vol 1, p70-71.

282 Equiano, *Interesting Narrative*, vol 1, p71.

283 Equiano, *Interesting Narrative*, vol 1, p71-72.

284 Equiano, *Interesting Narrative*, vol 1, p114.

285 Equiano, *Interesting Narrative*, vol 1, p216-217.

286 Equiano, *Interesting Narrative*, vol 1, p243-244.

287 Equiano, *Interesting Narrative*, vol 2, p11-12.

288 Equiano, *Interesting Narrative*, vol 2, p13-14.

289 Equiano, *Interesting Narrative*, vol 2, p22.

290 Equiano, *Interesting Narrative*, vol 1, p207.

291 Equiano, *Interesting Narrative*, vol 1, p208.

[292] Equiano, *Interesting Narrative*, vol 1, p207.

[293] Equiano, *Interesting Narrative*, vol 1, p223.

[294] Equiano, *Interesting Narrative*, vol 1, p223-224.

[295] Equiano, *Interesting Narrative*, vol1, p43.

[296] Equiano, *Interesting Narrative*, vol 1, p224-225.

[297] Walvin, *Black Ivory* xv.

[298] Equiano, *Interesting Narrative*, vol 2, p252.

[299] Cugoano, *Thoughts and Sentiments*, p9.

[300] Cugoano, *Thoughts and Sentiments*, p9.

[301] Cugoano, *Thoughts and Sentiments*, p10.

[302] Cugoano, *Thoughts and Sentiments*, p12.

[303] Cugoano, *Thoughts and Sentiments*, p12.

[304] Cugoano, *Thoughts and Sentiments*, p111.

[305] Cugoano, *Thoughts and Sentiments*, p97.

[306] Cugoano, *Thoughts and Sentiments*, p93.

[307] Cugoano, *Thoughts and Sentiments*, p127.

[308] Cugoano, *Thoughts and Sentiments*, p125.

[309] Cugoano, *Thoughts and Sentiments*, p125.

[310] Cugoano, *Thoughts and Sentiments*, p146.

[311] Cugoano, *Thoughts and Sentiments*, p22.

[312] Cugoano, *Thoughts and Sentiments*, p22.

[313] Cugoano, *Thoughts and Sentiments*, 1791 edition. Reprinted in Edwards (ed.) *Thoughts and Sentiments*, pxiii.

[314] Cugoano, *Thoughts and Sentiments*, 1791 edition.

[315] Cugoano, *Thoughts and Sentiments*, 1791 edition.

[316] Cugoano, *Thoughts and Sentiments*, p144.

[317] Cugoano, *Thoughts and Sentiments*, p145.

Chapter 7:
Concluding Remarks

[318] Fryer, *Staying Power*, p166.

Postscript:
Equiano's Nigerian Origin Discovered?

[319] Equiano, *Interesting Narratives*, p1-2.

[320] Walvin, *Black Ivory*, p25.

[321] Equiano, *Interesting Narrative*, vol 1, p18.

[322] Edwards, *The Life of Olaudah Equiano*, pxxii.

[323] Acholonu, *The Igbo Roots of Olaudah Equiano*, p3.

[324] The key problem is the replacement of the letter "e" with "i". If as Acholonu argues, this is a mistake Equiano makes in his spelling of Igbo names (so "Essaka" is really "Isseke") then one wonders why she did not assume Equiano has also spelled his own name, "Equiano", wrongly, since it also begins with "E". A consistent change of "e" to "I" would mean that "Equiano" would become "iquiano" of "Ikwealua". However, if this were the case, then the family Acholonu tracked down, the Ekwealua family, would no longer qualify as a possible origin for Equiano. It would appear that Acholonu has not followed a consistent argument in her dealings with the two names "Essaka" and "Equiano" which are central to her case.

[325] Edwards, *The Life of Olaudah Equiano*, pxxiii.

[326] Ugwu, *Change is Possible*, p68.

Printed in the United Kingdom
by Lightning Source UK Ltd.
119253UK00001B/85-189